# GOD'S ROADMAP FOR MAN:
## *The 7 Feasts of Israel*

by
Jim Kelly

# DEDICATION

To my grandchildren and great-grandchildren: Lynn, Mark, Robbie, Alicia, John, Jacob, Chase, and those not born yet: a dedication, a scripture, and a condensed statement of what I've learned are the most important things in life.

*But seek ye first the kingdom of God, and his righteousness; and all these things shall be added unto you.*

(Matthew 6:33 AV)

**Know Jesus, Know Peace.
No Jesus, No peace.**

# TABLE OF CONTENTS

# THE 7 FEASTS OF ISRAEL ( LEVITICUS 23 )

THE SPRING FEASTS ( The Former Rain ) FULL-FILLED

- Pesach / Passover
- Hag HaMatzah / Unleavened Bread
- Bikkurim / Firstfruits
- Shavuot / Pentecost / Weeks / First Trump

THE FALL FEASTS ( The Latter Rain ) YET TO BE FULLFILLED

- Rosh Ha' Shana / Feast of Trumpets / Last Trump
- Yom Kippur / Day of Atonement / Great Trump
- Sukkot / Tabernacles / Booths

THE PILGRIM FEASTS ( Deut. 16:16 ) Requires the presence of every able-bodied Jewish male in Jerusalem to observe the feast.

- Pesach / Passover
- Shavuot / Pentecost
- Sukkot / Tabernacles

# AUTHOR'S NOTES

It was late in life that I discovered the significance of the Jewish culture and history upon me as a Gentile Christian. I was born in the late 1930's, became a believer in Jesus Christ as my Lord and Savior when I was 12 years old, and attended church since my teen-age years. The church atmosphere in those days just after World War II was bordering on being anti-Semitic. I had never heard of the term "Messianic Jew" or a Jew that acknowledged Jesus Christ as the Messiah. In the "Bible Belt" of the Southern United States, no one I knew of studied Jewish culture or history because, after all, the Jews had rejected Jesus. It was much later in life that I came to the realization that my Lord Jesus Christ was and is a Jewish Rabbi. I also came to realize that woven into the Jew's Old Testament are types and shadows of the New Testament. It is all one book. Sixty-six books written by some 40 different scribes over thousands of years but with only one real author: The Holy Spirit. It has been said that the **Old Testament is the New Testament concealed** and **the New Testament is the Old Testament revealed**.

I went into prison ministry later in life and began a regular teaching schedule. As I prepared my lessons, I began to pick up bits and pieces of the significance of the Feasts of Israel. I became fascinated with this study. Some years back, my wife Josie and I were fortunate enough to get to go to Israel on a Bible study tour. It opened up a new world for me in my study of the feasts and of Jewish culture. I have taught on the feasts now for some 10 or 12 years and given programs at area churches as well as my teachings through the prison ministry. My teachings on the feasts have grown from a simple lesson, to an overhead projector presentation, to a Power Point presentation and now this book.

My research has lead me to several Messianic Jewish teachers such as the late Zola Levitt of Zola Levitt Ministries, Edward Chumney through the Messianic Jewish Movement, Steven Ger of Sojurner Ministries, and Mitch and Zhava Glasner with Jews For Jesus. I also gained much insight through several Gentile writers such as: Chuck Missler of Koinonia House Inc., Richard Booker of Sounds of The Trumpet, John Hagee of John Hagee Ministries and many other writers both Jew and Gentile. I do not mean to imply that all these writers agree with every point I make in this book or even agree among themselves on every point. Each one, however, made valuable contributions to my conclusions and understanding of the feasts.

Nothing in this material is meant to suggest that we, as Gentile believers in our Lord Jesus Christ, must celebrate the Seven Feasts God gave to the Jews in Leviticus 23. However, I find nothing in the scriptures that would suggest that we could not celebrate them if we wanted to. The blessing for the Gentile believer in studying these feasts is seeing God's plan for both the Jew and the Gentile in the symbolism and history of these feasts. Without looking at the Jewish culture and history of these feasts, we can never understand how they portray God's work with us as well as the Jews.

When you study this material suggesting the Seven Feasts are a model of when future events may occur, be careful you don't get caught up in "date setting." That is not the point of this study and we should be wary of falling into this trap.

Jesus said:

*But of that day and hour knoweth no [man], no, not the angels of heaven, but my Father only. But as the days of Noah [were], so shall also the coming of the Son of man be.*
(Matthew 24:36-37 AV)

The Feasts also are a model of the development of a baby as discovered a few years ago by Zola Levitt and included in this study. If you align the first month of a woman's pregnancy with the first month of the Jewish Religious Calendar, there is major development of the child on exactly the day of each of the feasts. Although the doctor and the mother may know when the time of delivery is very close, we could truly say, "No man knoweth the day or the hour when the child will be born." Could that be the message Jesus is telling us in the Matthew 24 passage above? "Know and be aware by the signs around you that the time is near, but leave the details to God."

In Daniel 12:4 the angel tells Daniel:

*But thou, O Daniel, shut up the words, and seal the book, [even] to the time of the end: many shall run to and fro, and knowledge shall be increased.*
(Daniel 12:4 AV)

And again in Daniel 12:9:

*And he said, Go thy way, Daniel: for the words [are] closed up and sealed till the time of the end.*
(Daniel 12:9 AV)

This would seem to indicate to me that understanding might be unsealed in the end times when, "many shall run to and fro, and knowledge shall be increased." This seems to be an exact description of the age we are living in.

Also in Amos 3:7 the prophet wrote:

*Surely the Lord GOD will do nothing, but he revealeth his secret unto his servants the prophets.*
(Amos 3:7 AV)

Could these modern-day prophets such as these that I've studied be the ones to whom God is revealing the secrets of the Feasts?

In Acts 17 is the story of Paul's visit to Berea. In verse 11 the writer, Luke, says:

*These were more noble than those in Thessalonica, in that they received the word with all readiness of mind, and searched the scriptures daily, whether those things were so.*
(Acts 17:11 AV)

My charge to you is to be like a Berean. Receive the Word readily and search the scriptures daily to see if these things are true.

If the dates aren't the point of this study, what is the purpose?

The purpose is to show you that, before the foundations of this world were laid, God had a plan for His Work with man. When the Old Testament was written down, this Plan was shadowed and symbolized in every story, every name, every law, every ordinance, every letter, every punctuation mark, and even the spaces between the letters of His Word. Some of this plan is revealed through these feasts.

That is what I believe Jesus meant when He said in Matthew:

> *Think not that I am come to destroy the law, or the prophets: I am not come to destroy, but to fulfill. For verily I say unto you, Till heaven and earth pass, one jot or one title shall in no wise pass from the law, till all be fulfilled.*
> (Matthew 5:17-18 AV)

The purpose is to show you that down through the ages, nothing happened by accident. God has had everything under complete control even to the point of making events happen on the exact anniversary in advance of a day when some more important event will happen in the future.

My purpose is to enlarge the image of God you have in you so you may more easily believe that if God can manage the events of the world, He can surely handle your problems.

Jim Kelly
2007

# INTRODUCTION

Israel and the Jewish people celebrate many feasts. At almost any time of the year, they are either celebrating a feast, getting ready to celebrate a feast, or ending the celebration of a feast. Many of these feasts are in memory of some event that happened in the history of the Jews and are very important to the Jews, but they are historical rather than scripturally based celebrations. Do not confuse these "lesser" feasts with the 7 major feasts commanded by God for the Jewish people to observe that are set forth in Leviticus 23.

## What are the 7 Feasts of the Lord in Leviticus 23?

Leviticus 23 is the first mention of the Feasts of Israel in the Old Testament. The whole chapter deals with the Feasts but for now let's just look at the beginning and ending of the chapter.

> *And the LORD spake unto Moses, saying, Speak unto the children of Israel, and say unto them, Concerning the feasts of the LORD, which ye shall proclaim to be holy convocations, even these are my feasts...*
> *And Moses declared unto the children of Israel the feasts of the LORD.*
>
> (Leviticus 23:1-2, 44 AV)

The Apostle Paul, a devout Jew who was educated in the Jewish faith and customs at the feet of Gamaliel[1] before meeting the Lord Jesus on the road to Damascus, had this to say of the feasts and holy days in Colossians 2:16 & 17.

> *Let no man therefore judge you in meat, or in drink, or in respect of an holyday[2] or of the new moon[3], or of the sabbath days[4]:"*
> *Which are a shadow of things to come; but the body is of Christ.*
>
> (Colossians 2:16-17 AV)

## Are the 7 Feasts A Road Map?

The conclusion from Colossians 2:16 & 17 would thus be that Paul was telling the Colossians and us that the feasts were a shadow of things to come. In other words, the feasts, new month celebrations, and sabbaths of the Jews are prophecy or patterns or maybe even a road map of God's work with man.

Is that the right conclusion? How do we check it out? Let's look at what the Word says.

> *This [is] the third [time] I am coming to you. In the mouth of two or three witnesses shall every word be established.*
>
> (2 Corinthians 13:1 AV)

Also in Matthew 18:16, 1 Timothy 5:19, Hebrews 10:28.

The principle here is what I call the law of two or three witnesses. If we have reached the correct conclusion from Paul's statement in Colossians, we should find other evidence of it in the Word. We will check that out.

It is also a common belief among Jewish Rabbis that the 7 Feasts in Leviticus 23 are fixed appointments between God and His Chosen People. What is a fixed appointment? Here is an example:

If you had a fixed appointment with your doctor planned months or even years in advance, would you expect your doctor to show up if you kept these appointments? Of course you would.

The Jews have the same expectation about their 7 Feasts. They expect God to show up. Can we find evidence in the Word that God is showing up exactly on these 7 feast days as the Jews expect?

Let's start with some well known historical events in both the Old and New Testaments and see how they relate to these 7 Feasts of Leviticus 23. Before we begin, however, let's look at what determines a day from a scriptural perspective because that will help us determine exactly when a feast day begins and ends.

We Gentiles tend to have a different idea of the beginning and ending of a day than the one described in the Word. Our day begins and ends at midnight but the Word says repeatedly in Genesis 1 that the "evening and the morning" were the first day and the second day and so on.

The common interpretation of this scripture by the Jewish Rabbis is that a day begins at twilight or more exactly with the appearance of the first star and ends at that same time on the following evening. If you take a trip to Israel today, you'll find that everything closes down for the weekly Sabbath on what we would call Friday evening at twilight and does not come to life again until Saturday evening twilight at the appearance of the first star. That method also determines the beginning and ending of the Feast days.

Now let's look for evidence of a pattern or road map by comparing the dates of well known events of the Old and New Testaments with the dates of the 7 Feasts.

**The first feast of the year on the 14th of the Jewish month of Nisan. Each feast has several names:**

**Passover or Pesach. (Leviticus 23:5) All this happened on the first Passover day (evening and morning):**

## Old Testament

- The lamb without spot or blemish was slain.

- It was killed at the 9th hour or at 3 PM our time. (Literally "between the two evenings.")

- It was cooked and eaten in a specified way. (No bones broken.)

- The blood of the lamb was applied to the doorpost of each house.

- The Lord passed over that house and did not strike the firstborn dead.

- The Jewish people were free to leave Egypt and bondage.[5]

Jesus (our Perfect Lamb) was crucified on the **exact** anniversary of that date thousands of years later. During the "evening and morning" of that day:

## New Testament

- He ate the Passover meal with His disciples.

- They left the upper room after it was dark.

- He was arrested during the night.

- He was scourged. (Blood was shed.)

- He was crucified. (More blood was shed but no bones were broken.)

- At "about the 9th hour", or at 3 PM our time, He died.

- His Blood, when applied by faith in His Death, Burial and Resurrection, over the doorposts of our lives, pays the penalty for our sins and God "passes over" us with His Judgment.

- We are free to leave the bondage of sin behind us. [6]

## Feast 2

**Unleavened bread or Hag HaMatzah (Leviticus 23: 6) Begins on the 15th of the Jewish month of Nisan and lasts 7 days.**

## Old Testament

When the Jews left Egypt they could not use leavening, or the ingredients to make bread rise, in their bread because they were traveling and the process to make bread rise required that it sit undisturbed for a period of time. When they were traveling, this was impossible.

Later they were told in Leviticus 23, to search their houses in observing this feast to rid the houses of all leaven. According to Jewish custom, the last crumbs of the leaven are swept up with a feather and a wooden spoon, wrapped in a linen cloth and taken to the temple to be burned.

Leaven is symbolic of sin. The search for leaven by the Jews in observing this feast symbolizes the search for and putting away of every crumb of sin in our lives.

## New Testament

That day at Calvary, Jesus took our every sin upon himself. The wooden spoon symbolizes the cross and the sweeping of the last crumbs into the wooden spoon to be wrapped in linen and burned symbolizes Jesus' body being wrapped in linen in the grave while his soul descended into hell. His body lay in the grave during the first few days of this feast.

## Feast 3

**First Fruits or Bikkurim (Leviticus 23:10-11)** A one-day Feast that always occurs on Sunday during the week of Unleavened Bread and can be 2 to 6 days following Passover. **It seems to have occurred exactly 3 days after Passover in years when important events occurred**. The following events happened exactly on that feast day:

## Old Testament

Red sea was split 3 days after the Jews observed the first Passover.[7]

## New Testament

Thousands of years later, Jesus arose 3 days after his death on Passover.[8]

## The 4th Feast and last of the Spring Feasts.

**Pentecost or Shavout or Feast of Weeks** (Leviticus 23:15-16) Always occurs on Sunday exactly 50 days after First Fruits or Bikkurim.

## Old Testament

Law was given to Moses on the mountain 50 days after the Red Sea was split.[9]

## New Testament

Thousands of years later, the Holy Spirit was given to the church 50 days after Jesus arose.[10]

Notice that for each Old Testament event that occurred on a Feast Day there is a New Testament fulfillment. Because of this, we say that these Feasts have been fulfilled.

These are the 4 Spring Feasts that would appear to represent God's work with mankind before this present time. **There are many more events not listed here that appear to have occurred exactly on the Spring Feast Days.** This is only the introduction and is not meant to list all the events that occurred on these days. We'll study these other lesser-known events in other chapters.

The remaining 3 Fall Feasts appear to have **not** been fulfilled yet but each of the Fall Feasts has definite themes that would suggest exactly what we could expect when they are fulfilled.

The first of the Fall Feasts themes suggest the event Christians call the **Rapture.**[11] The second of the Fall Feasts themes suggest the **second physical coming of the Messiah,**[12] and the third of the Fall Feasts themes suggest the **Millennial Rein of Messiah.**[13]

The Spring Feasts also suggest what the Old Testament Prophets call the **"time of the former rains"**[14] and the Fall Feasts suggest what they call the **"time of the latter rains."**[15]

If the Feasts are a roadmap to God's work with mankind, we should begin to see the overall outline of a map from the information presented so far. Every good map should show where we have been, where we are, and where we are going. Let's see how our map is beginning to shape up.

We have the 4 Spring Feasts that appear to have been fulfilled, followed by an indefinite period of time, and then the 3 Fall Feasts symbolizing events to come. Our present time, or the Church Age, or the Age of Grace, seems to be symbolized in the space between the Spring and Fall Feasts.

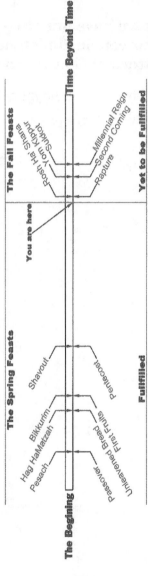

## It's your decision.

Keep this question in mind as we dig deeper in our study:

**Do you think we have our "two or three witnesses" to support our conclusion of the 7 Feasts being a road map or pattern of God's work with man?**

I believe we do but you are the jury. Keep reading; there is more evidence to present.

# INTRODUCTION ENDNOTES

1.  Acts 22:3

2.  The word translated as "holyday" in Colossians 2:16 (AV) is described in Strong's #1859 as the Greek word eorth heorte heh-or-tay'. In the King James Version (KJV) also called the Authorized Version (AV), this Greek word is translated by the translators as "feast" 26 times and as "holy day" 1 time.

It is defined by Strong's as: "a feast day, festival".

3.  The Greek word translated as "new moon" in Colossians 2:16 (AV) is Strong's #3561 noumhnia noumenia noo-may-nee'-ah or    neomhnia neomenia ne-o-may-nee'-a  It's found 1 time in the New Testament and defined by Strong's as:

1) new moon

1a) of the Jewish festival of the new moon

4.  The Greek word translated as "sabbath days" in Colossians 2:16 (AV) is Strongs # 4521 sabbaton sabbaton sab'-bat-on  It's found 68 times in the New Testament AV and translated as: sabbath day 37, sabbath 22, week 9.

It's defined by Strong's as:

1) the seventh day of each week which was a sacred festival on which the Israelites were required to abstain from all work

1a) the institution of the sabbath, the law for keeping holy every seventh day of the week

1b) a single sabbath, sabbath day

2) seven days, a week

5.  Exodus 12.

6.  From numerous passages in Matthew, Mark, Luke and John.

7.  Historical teaching of Jewish Rabbis. Alluded to in Exodus 5:3 and 3:18: "And they shall hearken to thy voice: and thou shalt come, thou and the elders of Israel, unto the king of Egypt, and ye shall say unto him, The LORD God of the Hebrews hath met with us: and now let us go, we beseech thee, three days' journey into the wilderness, that we may sacrifice to the LORD our God." (Exodus 3:18 AV)

8.  Matthew 12:40  For as Jonas was three days and three nights in the whale's belly; so shall the Son of man be three days and three nights in the heart of the earth.

9.  Historical teaching of Jewish Rabbis. Exodus 19:1, 10-17. Edward Chumney ,*The Seven Festivals of the Messiah.*© 1994,Destiny Image, Shippenburg, PA p. 74

10.  Acts 2

11. Zola Levitt, *The Seven Feasts of Israel,* © 1979. Dallas, TX. p12-13.

12. Edward Chumney, *The Seven Festivals of the Messiah.* © 1994, Destiny Image, Shippenburg, PA. p.150-154.

13. Edward Chumney, *The Seven Festivals of the Messiah.* © 1994, Destiny Image, Shippenburg, PA p. 167.

14.

> *Then shall we know, if we follow on to know the LORD: his going forth is prepared as the morning; and he shall come unto us as the rain, as the latter and former rain unto the earth.*
>
> (Hosea 6:3 AV)

> *Be glad then, ye children of Zion, and rejoice in the LORD your God: for he hath given you the former rain moderately, and he will cause to come down for you the rain, the former rain, and the latter rain in the first month.*
>
> (Joel 2:23 AV)

15.

> *Ask ye of the LORD rain in the time of the latter rain; so the LORD shall make bright clouds, and give them showers of rain, to every one grass in the field.*
>
> (Zechariah 10:1 AV)

# CHAPTER ONE

If the feasts were and are a prophetic road map as I believe they are, that is not the only thing we can learn from a study of them. God's Word has such depth that every time we think we understand it, the Holy Spirit shows us another, deeper layer. It is much like peeling an onion. When you remove one layer, there's another under it and another under that one until you get to the core. We have just begun to discover outer layers, and are not even close to the core, as far as God's Word is concerned. Let's look at some of the other things, other than being a road map that the feasts are.

## THE FEASTS WERE VISUAL AIDS TO THE JEWS TO PREPARE THEM FOR THE COMING OF JESUS THE MESSIAH.

We live in an age when visual aids are an accepted teaching practice. From the kindergarten teacher to the executive presenting a new program or sales presentation, visual aids get the point across. Pictures, slides, overhead projections, DVD's, CD's, projected computer charts and images are all used by competent teachers in our times to get an idea across.

The Feasts were God's Visual Aids to teach the Jews about the coming of Jesus the Messiah and to reveal to them the order of events in His Work with mankind. For centuries, He had them acting out the story of Jesus and then Jesus followed the script perfectly when He came. Let's look at the teachings of Passover, the first of the 7 feasts described in Leviticus 23.

In about 1446 BC, [16] on the night before Moses was to lead the Israelite nation out of Egypt and bondage, the Israelite nation observed the first Passover as they had been instructed by God. They had been told to select a male lamb for each household without blemish and to separate him and take him into their own household on the 10th day of the month. The lamb was to remain in each household until the 14th of the month and "between the evenings" or at 3 PM our time, the lamb was to be killed in a certain way. The lamb's body was to be drained of all blood, skinned, disemboweled and prepared for cooking. No bone could be broken in either the preparation or the eating of the lamb. The lamb's body was then roasted while attached to a pole or spit with a cross stick to hold open the ribs for cooking.

While the lamb was cooking, the blood that had been drained from his body was to be painted over the doorpost or entry to every house by the head of the household. The Israelites were told that the Lord Himself was coming across the land to judge Egypt and to strike the firstborn of every family dead but if the blood of the lamb was over the doorpost, the Lord would pass over that household and all would be safe.

They were also instructed in the way they were to eat the Passover lamb. It must be served with unleavened bread and bitter herbs. They were to eat the meal with their shoes on their feet, their staff in their hand, and their belongings packed to leave. They had to eat all of the lamb. There could be no leftovers.

To stress the importance of this feast, God told them that they were to observe this feast always on the anniversary of this night and to again stress the importance of this feast, had them completely change their calendar and make this the first month of the year from now on. [17]

For more than 14 centuries the Israelites observed this Passover Feast in the same manner understanding that the blood of a sacrificial lamb was a temporary covering for their sin and this temporary covering would cause God to "pass over" them with his judgment for another year. During that interval of time, prophets foretold that some day, God would provide a perfect Lamb who would pay the penalty for their sin once and for all.

Now let's examine how Jesus followed this script exactly in the events described in the New Testament.

The Jews were told to select a yearling lamb without blemish and to take the lamb into their household. Our Bible text doesn't tell us why, but Jewish tradition teaches that the main reason for taking the lamb into the household was so he could be examined to be sure he was without blemish. For 4 days each family examined the lamb for a fault or blemish.

In John 12:1 we are told:

*Then Jesus six days before the Passover came to Bethany, where Lazarus was which had been dead, whom he raised from the dead.*
(John 12:1 AV)

Verses 2-11 relate the events at Bethany that day.

Verse 12 tells us that:

*On the next day much people that were come to the feast, when they heard that Jesus was coming to Jerusalem, took branches of palm trees, and went forth to meet him, and cried, Hosanna: Blessed [is] the King of Israel that cometh in the name of the Lord.*
(John 12:12-13 AV)

The Passover was always on the 14th day of the first month of Nisan. John 12:1 is telling us that he arrived in Bethany on the 8th day of the month of Nisan. John 12:12 tells us that when He made what we call the "Triumphant Entry" into Jerusalem that day, it was the 9th day of Nisan. That night after twilight, it became the 10th of Nisan.

From the following verses, it is plain that Jesus presented Himself at the Temple in the following days and that the Jewish leaders examined God's Perfect Lamb. Pilate himself said, "I find no fault in him." The Old Testament script said that the lamb was to be examined from the 10th until the 14th of the month and the New Testament records that Jesus followed the script exactly. He was crucified on the 14th of the month and died at the 9th hour at exactly the time decreed for killing the Passover lambs.

For 4 days preceding the crucifixion, the Jews examined Him thoroughly.

His body lay in the grave wrapped in linen during the first few days of the Feast of Unleavened Bread. His body in the grave represented a seed planted in the ground from which new life would spring. Leaven symbolized sin and God had put our sins upon Him to be buried forever.

> *For he hath made him [to be] sin for us, who knew no sin; that we might be made the righteousness of God in him.*
> (2 Corinthians 5:21 AV)

He arose on exactly the day the Jewish Priests presented the "Firstfruits" of the new harvest. He became the first of a new kind of creature that has been raised from death. By faith in His Death, Burial and Resurrection, we are also raised from spiritual death and become a new creature.

> *Therefore if any man [be] in Christ, [he is] a new creature: old things are passed away; behold, all things are become new.*
> (2 Corinthians 5:17 AV)

> *But now Christ is risen from the dead, and has become the firstfruits of those who have fallen asleep.*
> (1 Corinthians 15:20 AV)

The Jews were set free from Egypt's bondage. The sacrifice of the Perfect Lamb (Jesus) that day at Calvary set all mankind free from sin's bondage. When any man or woman accepts Jesus Christ as Savior, that person becomes a new creature, born again by faith in Jesus'

Death, Burial and Resurrection, and is set free from the bondage of sin.

> *If the Son therefore shall make you free, ye shall be free indeed.*
>
> (John 8:36 AV)

> *For the law of the Spirit of life in Christ Jesus hath made me free from the law of sin and death.*
> (Romans 8:2 AV)

> *Stand fast therefore in the liberty wherewith Christ hath made us free, and be not entangled again with the yoke of bondage.*
> (Galatians 5:1 AV)

## Patterns and Suggestive Symbolism in the Feasts

As we begin our study of the feasts, we cannot help but notice that there is much symbolism in everything pertaining to the feasts.  I am unable to point out all the symbolism and patterns of the feasts, because no man can know all they suggest, but I can point out some things that might be suggestive of future events or of patterns that are followed in the Old and New Testaments.

## God's Perfect Order:  The Sevens

It is no accident that the **7** Feasts of Israel begin in the first month and end in the **seventh** month.  In the scriptures, the number **7** has been called "God's Number."  It also signifies fullness or completeness.[18]  The study of **sevens** in the scriptures yields an astounding pattern of the number **7** or it's multiples woven all through the Bible.

**34**

The study of the **7** Feasts has a woven-in pattern of **sevens** and multiples imbedded into the times of the feasts, the days of duration of the feasts, the number of sacrifices, the actions of the priests in carrying out the instructions, and probably many more patterns of **sevens** that we have not recognized.

I'll try to point out some of these patterns as we go through the study, but be sensitive to the Holy Spirit as we go through the material. I can only present the information. He alone can lead you to the truth and understanding of the material.[19]

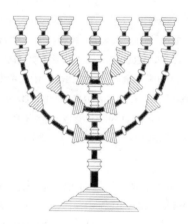

## The Menorah

The Menorah is the golden lamp stand that was part of the Jews Temple furniture. The Menorah is so woven into modern Jewish culture than an image of the Menorah is seen as a symbol of the present-day nation of Israel and is common on their official literature.

The Menorah has a central main vertical upright with 3 branches on either side of the main upright. Each branch and the central main upright have a cup for holding olive oil and a wick for a total of **seven** lights.

When you look at the Menorah in the context of the 7 Feasts of Israel, you notice that there are 3 lights on the left, symbolizing the spring 3 Feasts in the first month. The three lights on the right symbolize the fall 3 Feasts in the **seventh** month. The central main upright light symbolizes the fourth feast in between the 3 spring and 3 fall feasts.[20]

God's perfect order of the 7's is woven into almost everything we know about God's work with man and especially in the Jewish culture. It is certainly evident in their measurement of time. God created the earth in 6 days and on the **7**th, He rested and called that day holy. He commanded the Jews to keep that **seventh** day of the week as a holy day or a Sabbath as a day of remembrance of what He had done.[21]

When the instructions are given in determining the feast of Pentecost/Shavuot/Feast of Weeks, the Jews are instructed to count off **seven** Sabbaths after Firstfruits and the next day will be Pentecost/Shavuot/Feast of Weeks. It always comes out to be 50 days but the instructions say to count **seven** Sabbaths and then it will be the next day. In other words, it is **7** weeks plus 1 day. [22]

The Spring Feasts are in the first month and the Fall Feasts are in the **seventh** month.

The Jews are commanded to let the land rest every **seventh** year.[23] When they are carried away to Babylon by Nebuchadnezzar, the Bible records the reason for their defeat as being that they did not keep the Sabbaths for the land.[24] When the Jews still did not repent after **70** years of captivity, God multiplied their sentence by **7** for a total of **490** years.[25] The history of the Jews as recorded in the Bible seems to be broken up into **490** year periods (70X7 years). Even the period prophesied by Daniel[26] as **70** weeks of years (70X7) is **490** years. It is broken down as 62+7 or 69 weeks of years (69X7) or **483** years and appears to have been fulfilled to the very day when Jesus rode the colt of the donkey into Jerusalem as recorded in John 12:12-13.[27] **Seven** years are missing from this **490** year period. Many believe that the **seventieth** week of this prophecy is the **seven** years of the period that the Bible calls the "Great Tribulation" and will make this period **490** years as well. The interval of time between the ending of the 69th week and the beginning of the **70**th week is thought to be the "Church Age" or the period of time we are in now.

The year after the **seventh** Sabbath for the land (7X7 or 49 years) is to be a Jubilee year. Notice that the pattern of counting years to determine a Jubilee year (49+1) is the same pattern as counting off the weeks to determine the 50 days between Firstfruits and Pentecost as shown above. In this Jubilee year all debts are forgiven, slaves are set free and returned to their families, and the entire year is a time of rejoicing. There is to be no sowing or reaping or work in the fields.[28]

Jesus was speaking about this year of Jubilee when he said in Luke 4:18-21:

**37**

> *The Spirit of the Lord is upon me, because he*
> *hath anointed me to preach the gospel to the poor;*
> *he hath sent me to heal the brokenhearted, to*
> *preach deliverance to the captives, and recovering*
> *of sight to the blind, to set at liberty them that are*
> *bruised, To preach the acceptable year of the*
> *Lord.* [29] *And he closed the book, and he gave it*
> *again to the minister, and sat down. And the eyes*
> *of all them that were in the synagogue were fas-*
> *tened on him. And he began to say unto them,*
> *This day is this scripture fulfilled in your ears.*

To Jesus's Jewish audience in the Synagogue that day, the "acceptable year of the Lord" from Isaiah that He spoke of, was understood to be a Jubilee year. They understood that only the Messiah could proclaim it. That is why they tried to throw Him over the cliff in the following verses.

These years of Jubilee that the Jews observed for centuries are a perfect picture of this present era that began with Jesus' Ministry, Death, and Resurrection. God had this age planned in advance for thousands of years and had the Jews acting out the events of this age every Jubilee year.

In other places in the Scriptures, even the casual reader will notice the frequency of the number **seven**. Some of the best known are: Solomon's building of the Temple **seven** years, and later in the book of Revelation the **seven** churches, **seven** seals, **seven** trumpets, **seven** bowls, **seven** stars etc.[30]

Jesus made **seven** statements from the cross. Jesus spoke **seven** times to the woman at the well and she responded six times (the number of man). Jacob served **seven** years for each of his wives. Through Joseph, God decreed **seven** years of plenty before the **seven** years of famine, the vision of Pharaoh had **seven** cows and **seven** heads of grain, Naaman was required to wash in the river **seven** times, Elisha's servant looked **seven** times for the appearance of rain, Nebuchadnezzar's insanity lasted **seven** years, **seven** clean animals were taken into the ark, and on and on the examples go.

Genesis 1:1 when examined in the original Hebrew contains **seven** words. It is translated in the Authorized or King James Version as: "In the beginning God created the heaven and the earth."

It would be hard to miss the suggestion that **seven** is God's symbol of perfection and is woven throughout all the scriptures to a level we have not even discovered yet.

Mark Eastman, M.D. and Chuck Missler, in their book: "The Creator Beyond Space and Time," have the following to say about Jesus' lineage as shown in the first 17 verses of Matthew:

If we look at the first 17 verses of the New Testament (The Gospel of Matthew) which deals with a single principal subject: the genealogy of Jesus Christ, it contains 72 Greek vocabulary words in these initial 17 versus(*note; The verse divisions are man's allocation for convenience, added in the thirteenth-century A.D.). We find the following Heptadic (7) structure throughout these original Greek verses.

#1. The number of words which are nouns is exactly 56, or 7 x 8.

#2. The Greek word "the" occurs most frequently in the passage: exactly 56 times, or 7 x 8.

#3. Also, the number of different forms in which the article "the" occurs is exactly 7.

#4. There are two main sections in the passage: verse 1-11 and 12-17. In the first main section, the number of Greek vocabulary words used is 49, or 7 x 7.

#5. Of these 49 words, the number of those beginning with a vowel is 28, or 7 x 4.

#6. The number of words beginning with a consonant is 21, or 7 x 3.

#7. The total number of letters in these 49 words is exactly 266, or 7 x 38-exactly.

#8. The numbers of vowels among these 266 letters is 140, or 7 x 20.

#9. The number of consonants is 126, or 7 x 18-exactly.

#10. Of these 49 words, the number of words which occur more than once is 35, or 7 x 5.

#11. The number of words occurring only once is 14, or 7 x2.

#12. The number of words which occur in only one form is exactly 42, or 7 x 6.

#13. The number of words appearing in more than one form is also 7.

#14. The number of 49 Greek vocabulary words which are nouns is 42, or 7 x 6.

#15. The number of words which are not nouns is 7.

#16. Of the nouns, 35 are proper names, or 7 x 5.

#17. These 35 nouns are used 63 times, or 7 x 9.

#18. The number of male names is 28, or 7 x 4.

#19. These male names occur 56 times or 7 x 8.

#20. The number which are not male names is 7.

#21. Three women are mentioned-Tamar, Rahab, and Ruth. The number of Greek letters in these three names is 14, or 7 x 2.

#22. The number of compound nouns is 7.

#23. The number of Greek letters in these 7 nouns is 49, or 7 x 7.

#24. Only one city is named in this passage, Babylon, which in Greek contains exactly 7 letters. And on and on it goes."[31]

"By the way, the crucifixion of Jesus took place at Golgotha, elevation = 777 meters above sea level. What a coincidence."[32]

# CHAPTER ONE ENDNOTES

16. *The Strongest Strong's Exhaustive Concordance of the Bible*, James Strong LLD, STD-© 2001 by Zondervan.

17. Exodus 12.

18. Vine's *Expository Dictionary of Biblical Words.* Thomas Nelson Publishers. 1985 Edition.

19.

> *But the Comforter, which is the Holy Ghost, whom the Father will send in my name, he shall teach you all things, and bring all things to your remembrance, whatsoever I have said unto you.*
> (John 14:26 AV)

> *Howbeit when he, the Spirit of truth, is come, he will guide you into all truth: for he shall not speak of himself; but whatsoever he shall hear, that shall he speak: and he will shew you things to come.*
> (John 16:13 AV)

20. Chuck Missler Tape series: The Feasts of Israel, Tape 1.

21. Ex. 20:8

22. Lev. 23:15-16.

23. Lev. 25:4

24. 2 Chronicles 36:20-21

25. Lev. 26:18

26. Daniel 9:25-27

27. Sir Robert Anderson, *The Coming Prince*, Kregel Publications, Box 2607,Grand Rapids, MI 49501

28. Lev. 25:8-15

29. Is. 61:1-2

30. Mark Eastman, M.D. and Chuck Missler, *The Creator Beyond Space and Time*, © 1996 The Word For Today. p. 115, 118-122 -R. McCormack, *The Heptadic Structure of Scripture*, Marshall Bothers Ltd., London, 1923: E.W. Bullinger, *Numbers of the Scriptures*: F.W. Grant, The Numerical Bible (7 Vols.): Brown, Ordo Saeculoreium, et al. -Ivan Panin (various works), Bible Numerics, P.O. Box 206, Waubaushene, Ontario, L0K-2C0.

31. *Creator Beyond Time and Space* by Mark Eastman, M.D. and Chuck Missler, © 1996 by The Word For Today. Reprinted by permission of The Word For Today, P.O. Box 8000, Costa Mesa, CA 92628, www.twft.com.

32. *Creator Beyond Time and Space* by Mark Eastman, M.D. and Chuck Missler, © 1996 by The Word For Today. Reprinted by permission of The Word For Today, P.O. Box 8000, Costa Mesa, CA 92628, www.twft.com.

# CHAPTER TWO

TYPES OR MODELS IN THE FEASTS AND
ELSEWHERE THAT SUGGEST A PRE-TRIBULA-
TION RAPTURE OF THE CHURCH

The Church, which I define as all born-again believers
in our Lord Jesus Christ, has many different beliefs about
the timing of the event spoken of in 1 Thessalonians 4:13-
17:

> *But I would not have you to be ignorant, brethren,
> concerning them which are asleep, that ye sorrow
> not, even as others which have no hope. For if we
> believe that Jesus died and rose again, even so
> them also which sleep in Jesus will God bring with
> him. For this we say unto you by the word of the
> Lord, that we which are alive and remain unto the
> coming of the Lord shall not prevent them which
> are asleep. For the Lord himself shall descend
> from heaven with a shout, with the voice of the
> archangel, and with the trump of God: and the
> dead in Christ shall rise first: Then we which are
> alive and remain shall be caught up together with
> them in the clouds, to meet the Lord in the air: and
> so shall we ever be with the Lord.*

The same event is mentioned in 1 Corinthians 15:51-52:

> *Behold, I shew you a mystery; We shall not all sleep, but we shall all be changed, In a moment, in the twinkling of an eye, at the last trump: for the trumpet shall sound, and the dead shall be raised incorruptible, and we shall be changed.*

Christians commonly call this "catching away of the Church" the Rapture. The timing of this event is not specified in so many words in either the Old or the New Testaments so there are several differing opinions of when this will take place among respected Bible scholars. Proponents of each view have good reasons for their conclusions based on their understanding of the Scriptures. It would be safe to say that each of the views is an opinion of someone and no one really knows the correct answer except God. It could even be that all views are wrong.

Some of the main beliefs are:

## PRE-TRIBULATION:

The belief that the Church will be caught away before the times described in the Bible as the seven year period of the Great Tribulation.

## MID-TRIBULATION:

The belief that the Church will be caught away at the midpoint of the seven years of the Great Tribulation.

## POST-TRIBULATION:

The belief that the Church will be here on earth for all the trials and judgments of the seven years of the Great Tribulation.

Because of the controversy and uncertainty of the many views of when the Rapture will occur, many Christians today have developed another view which is jokingly described as Pan-Tribulation.

## PAN-TRIBULATION:

The belief that we do not know when the Rapture will happen but we believe God will cause it all to "pan out".

I really cannot go into any detailed study of when the Rapture will occur without revealing my beliefs on the subject. I'm a pre-tribulation proponent and my views may be wrong by your standards but I would like to show you what my belief is based on. I have heard many views of beliefs about the Rapture that hinge on what some famous scholar or pastor believes. My views are not based on some seminary's views or some professor's views but are based on what I believe are patterns or suggestions from the Scriptures and are available to anyone who begins to dig into the Word with the leadership of the Holy Spirit.

## THE SEVEN FEASTS OF ISRAEL SUGGEST A PRE-TRIB RAPTURE

As I stated earlier in the introduction, the seven feasts begin in the Jewish month of Nisan, which is about the same time as our month of March or April depending on the year. The first three feasts are in Nisan and the fourth feast is counted off as 50 days from the third feast. It occurs in the Jewish month of Sivan. Then there is an interval of several months and the three remaining fall feasts all occur in the Jewish month of Tishiri, which is in the September/October months of our calendar.

Each of the seven feasts has a definite theme or suggestion in Jewish history and in the Hebrew language.

1. **Passover**: The day the perfect lamb was killed in Egypt and the blood was applied to the doorpost of each house to protect the occupants from the Death Angel.

This was the first feast that was fulfilled by Jesus in his earthly ministry. Thousands of years later, He was crucified on Passover. Symbolically we apply His Blood over the doorposts of our life when we accept Him as Lord and Savior.

**Theme:** The Blood obtains forgiveness.

2. **Unleavened Bread**: In the actions performed by the Jews in observance of this feast, leaven, which is a symbol of sin, is diligently sought out and removed from the house. Thousands of years later, Jesus, who had no sin, took our sins upon Himself, and lay in the tomb during the first three days of the Feast of Unleavened Bread.

**Theme**: Sin (leaven) is to be searched out of our lives and buried.

*48*

**3. First Fruits**: The day that the Jews brought the first fruits of the Promised Land and offered them to God at the Tabernacle. Thousands of years later, Jesus tomb was found empty on that exact morning and He became the firstborn or first fruits of those that were once dead and are now alive. He symbolized how you and I were once dead without Christ and become alive through putting our faith in Him.

**Theme**: A new beginning, the old man was dead and buried and is now replaced by the new creature.

**4. Pentecost/Feast of Weeks**: Jewish tradition recognizes this feast day as the exact day that Moses received the Law from God on the mountain. Thousands of years later, the book of Acts records this as the exact day that the Holy Spirit was given to the Church.

**Theme:** The Old Testament or Covenant is replaced by the New.

**5. Feast of Trumpets/Rosh Hashanah**: Believed by the Jews as the exact day Messiah (not necessarily Jesus) will return.

The Orthodox Jews, you see, do not believe Jesus was and is the Messiah of the Old Testament and are waiting for the first coming of their Messiah. Christians, however, believe Jesus was and is the Messiah of both the New and the Old Testaments and that this will be His second appearance. Since the Orthodox Jew does not read or recognize the New Testament as the Word of God, their perception of the Messiah is only from what Christians call the

**49**

Old Testament scriptures. We know from the New Testament that when Jesus the Messiah comes again the graves will open and those who are alive will be caught up to meet him in the air at the blast of the last trump.[33] The similarities between the themes the Jews associate with this feast and the teaching of the New Testament about Jesus' second appearance are startling.

**Theme:** The Jew's trumpets on this feast day symbolize the **Coronation of the Messiah**. In fact, one of the other names for this feast day is the "**Last Trump**". It is also believed by the Jews to be the day of the **great resurrection** (natzal[34]) when the graves will be opened. This feast day has not been fulfilled by Jesus as the first four feasts have been.

6.  **Yom Kippur/Day of Atonement**: Believed by the Jews to be the exact day when Messiah will come and set up His Earthly Kingdom. It is the one day of the year when the High Priest, after much cleansing, enters into the Holy of Holies in the Temple to present the sacrifice for sin for the people. They believe the Messiah will come on this day to present the sacrifice and set up His earthly kingdom.

**Theme**: The **physical** coming of the Messiah to set up His earthly Kingdom. Not fulfilled.

7.  **Sukkot/Feast of Tabernacles**: Believed by the Jews to be the exact day when the thousand year reign of Messiah will begin.

**Theme**: The beginning of the Millennial Reign of Messiah. Not fulfilled.

The themes and fulfillment by Jesus of the Seven Feasts of Israel suggest also the order in which these end-time events will occur. Jesus fulfilled the first four in the exact order of the feasts. I think we can assume He will fulfill the final three feasts in the exact order of the feasts. To me, that means the next event will be the rapture or catching away of the Church before the Great Tribulation.

If we apply the law of two or three witnesses to this type or suggestion found in the 7 Feasts of Israel, are there other types or suggestions in the scriptures to back up this type or suggestion of a pre-tribulation rapture? Yes, I know of several:

# PRE-TRIB PATTERN # 2- THE FLOOD

One of the major events in the Old Testament is the flood story in Genesis Chapter 6, 7 and 8. It is a story that is familiar to old and young alike. Rather than go into this well-known story detail by detail, let's back off and look at the story of the flood as an overview. The flood was sent upon the earth by God as a judgment. God gave the sign of the rainbow as His promise that the earth would never be destroyed again by water. Peter tells us, however, that there is another destruction of the earth coming and this time it will be by fire.[35]

If you examine the Bible carefully, you'll find that every passage was written to either the Jews, the world, or the church. Is there typology or symbolism in the story of the flood? Yes there is.

Many sermons have been preached on how Jesus is symbolized by the ark. For example:

One door = one way to be saved;

When God closed the door, no one else could enter=You must decide in this life to accept Jesus before the door of death is closed;

Only a few were saved = Jesus said:

*Because strait is the gate, and narrow is the way, which leadeth unto life, and few there be that find it.*

(Matthew 7:14 AV)

And the types go on an on.

With the fact in mind that the Bible is written to three groups of people, let's examine the flood story and see if we can identify a type or symbol of each of these groups of people we mentioned above: the Jews, the world, and the Church.

Type #1- Noah and his family. They symbolize the remnant of the Jewish people that were preserved through the flood and that will be preserved in the future tribulations.

Type #2- Those who missed the boat. They symbolize the secular world that do not believe today and will not believe in the future judgment.

That leaves us looking for a symbol of the Church. Who or what group of people symbolize the Church in the flood story? Let's dig a little deeper.

When we look back at Noah's lineage in Genesis 5, we find a perfect example of the pre-tribulation rapture of the Church in Noah's great grandfather, Enoch.

*And Enoch walked with God: and he was not; for God took him.*

(Genesis 5:24 AV)

*By faith Enoch was translated that he should not see death; and was not found, because God had translated him: for before his translation he had this testimony, that he pleased God.*

(Hebrews 11:5 AV)

Enoch did not die, but was "raptured" or as Hebrews says, "translated". This happened well before the flood. I believe this is a perfect picture or type of what will happen to the Church in the future judgment and supports the pattern suggested in the 7 Feasts of Israel.

# PRE-TRIB PATTERN # 3
# THE DESTRUCTION OF
# SODOM AND GOMORRAH

Another of the major events of the Bible was the destruction of Sodom and Gomorrah as related in Genesis Chapters 18 and 19. Again, let's look at an overview of the story and then zoom in on certain details.

Abraham and his group of herders were camped at the "Oaks of Mamre"[36] when three men appeared walking toward Sodom and Gomorrah. One of them, whom scholars believe was a pre-incarnate appearance of our Lord Jesus Christ, talked with Abraham and Sarah as the men tarried while the meal Abraham had offered was being prepared. They revealed they were on their way to Sodom and Gomorrah to destroy it if they found it to be as wicked a city as had been reported.

Then came the part of the story when Abraham, who was the first Hebrew or Jew, began to bargain with the Lord about the fate of Sodom and Gomorrah:

"Will you destroy it if there are 50 righteous," Abraham began.

The Lord replied, "No. I will not destroy it if there are 50 righteous."

This discourse continued until they got to 10 and the Lord said He would not destroy it if there were 10.

Then the three left Abraham's camp walking toward Sodom and Gomorrah as Abraham watched them walk away.

What is the point of what I have related so far? Just this: I believe Abraham could have gone farther in bargaining with the Lord. Let me explain.

In Genesis 19:1 we discover that the other two "men" that appeared to Abraham were angels and the story finds them arriving at Sodom at evening and contacting Lot, Abraham's nephew. From here the story goes on to relate how the angels sought refuge at Lot's house from the wickedness of the men at Sodom. The angels struck the men of Sodom blind and told Lot and his family to leave the city because they (the angels) were going to destroy it. Then one of the angels made a statement that I think reveals God's instructions in times of judgment or destruction.

Then the angel told Lot.:

*Haste thee, escape thither; for I cannot do any thing till thou be come thither. Therefore the name of the city was called Zoar.*

(Genesis 19:22 AV)

It appears that the angel was saying that he could not bring any destruction or judgment upon Sodom and Gomorrah as long as there were any righteous present; even one.

That presents the next question: Why was Lot righteous? Here was a man who had chosen to live in the most wicked city in the world and not only live there but the Bible states that he was part of the government of that city.[37] How then could God count him as righteous? Yet Peter says in the New Testament:

*And delivered just Lot, vexed with the filthy conversation of the wicked.*

(2 Peter 2:7 AV)

How did Lot become just or righteous as Peter stated? From the information in the Bible, we can only answer that question by asking how Abraham, his uncle who also lived in that time frame, became righteous. We can answer that question with scripture:

*For what saith the scripture? Abraham believed God, and it was counted unto him for righteousness.*

(Romans 4:3 AV)

How did Abraham achieve righteousness?  Only through faith in God under the Old Testament.

How did Lot achieve righteousness?  Although we are not told in the Scripture, it must have been the same as Abraham; only through faith in God under the Old Testament.

How do you and I achieve righteousness?  Only through faith in God through Jesus Christ the Son under the New Testament.

> *But we are all as an unclean thing, and all our righteousnesses are as filthy rags; and we all do fade as a leaf; and our iniquities, like the wind, have taken us away.*
>
> (Isaiah 64:6 AV)

At the moment of our acceptance and confession of Jesus Christ the Son as our Savior, we give Him our clothes of sin and put on His clothes of righteousness. That's the only way we can become righteous.  Not by our good works or good life we live but only by our faith in Him. Through Jesus Christ the Son, however, we are the righteous.[38]

What is the conclusion we can draw from all this?  God's rules seem to be in this situation that no judgment or destruction will come until all the righteous have been removed.  In other words, this would indicate in future times, a pre-tribulation removal of all who are the righteous because of their faith in Jesus Christ the Son.  That's us: the Church.  You can stay for all the bad things of the Great Tribulation if you want to, but as for me and mine — we're outta here.

# PRE-TRIB PATTERN #4-THE FIERY FURNACE OF DANIEL

Again we go to another well known story from the Old Testament that is related in Daniel Chapter 3. Shadrach, Meshach, Abednego and Daniel were bright young Jewish men that Nebuchadnezzar, king of Babylon, captured when Israel was defeated. They were carried away to Babylon and in the course of time, became part of King Nebuchadnezzar's government. Shadrach, Meshach and Abednego are mentioned along with Daniel himself in passages in Daniel.

Chapter 3 of Daniel relates the story of how King Nebuchadnezzar built a golden statue of himself and issued a decree that at the time of music blast, all subjects of the kingdom would bow down to the statue under penalty of death. The story continues as Shadrach, Meshach and Abednego refuse to bow and are sentenced to burn in the fiery furnace. They are thrown into the fiery furnace and Nebuchadnezzar sees not only the three men he threw into the furnace, but a fourth man that he perceives as "the Son of God". When the three Hebrew men come out of the fire there is not a hair of their hair singed and not even the smell of smoke on their clothes.

That is an old familiar story that has been the subject of many good sermons and Bible studies. The question is, however, where was Daniel? In reality, he probably was gone to another part of the kingdom attending to affairs of state but we are not told that. We only know that he's missing in the entire story of the fiery furnace.

Could Daniel be a type of the Church? Could the fiery furnace be a type of the coming judgment? Could Shadrach, Meshach and Abednego be a type of the remnant of the Jews, who are protected through the fiery trials to come? If Daniel is a type of the Church, he is not there during the fiery trial. A pre-tribulation rapture would mean that the Church was not there also during the fiery trials to come and would also support the pattern set forth in the 7 Feasts of Israel.

# PRE-TRIB PATTERN #5-THE CONSTRUCTION OF THE BOOK OF REVELATION

The book of Revelation, at the end of the New Testament has much to say of end-time events. There are many opinions and beliefs on the meaning of much of this book. Let me show you one of the types in the very construction of the book that might point to a pre-tribulation rapture and support the pattern in the 7 Feasts of Israel.

According to my version of Strong's Exhaustive Concordance of the Bible, the Greek word "ekklesia", which is Strong's #1577, is used 18 times in the book of Revelation. It is translated into English as "Church".

Seventeen of the 18 occurrences of the Greek word "ekklesia" are found in the first 3 chapters of Revelation in the letters to the seven churches, etc. The only other place it is used in the book of Revelation is in Revelation 22:16 where it reflects back on the first three chapters. In other words, the Greek word for church is missing from the entire book of revelation after the first three chapters.

Why? What is the subject of Revelation after the first three chapters?

Let's look at Revelation 4:1 and 2:

*After this I looked, and, behold, a door was opened in heaven: and the first voice which I heard was as it were of a trumpet talking with me; which said, Come up hither, and I will shew thee things which must be hereafter. And immediately I was in the spirit: and, behold, a throne was set in heaven, and one sat on the throne.*

(Revelation 4:1-2 AV)

This is the point where John was caught up or "raptured". Could this type in the construction be telling us that after the events in the third chapter of Revelation, the Church is not present for all the other things revealed in the rest of the book of Revelation? If so, then this construction predicts a pre-tribulation rapture of the Church and supports the pattern of the 7 Feasts of Israel.

# CHAPTER TWO ENDNOTES

33. 1 Thessalonians 4:13-17, 1 Corinthians 15:51-52.

34. Edward Chumney, *The Seven Festivals of the Messiah.*© 1994, Destiny Image, Shippenburg, PA, p. 97-100

35. 2 Peter 3:7 & 3:12

36. Near present-day Hebron.

37. Genesis 19:1. The elders or city leaders sat in the gate.

38.

*But to him that worketh not, but believeth on him that justifieth the ungodly, his faith is counted for righteousness.*

(Romans 4:5 AV)

# CHAPTER THREE

**THE DEVELOPMENT OF A BABY AS COMPARED TO THE FEASTS OF ISRAEL**

One of the most amazing patterns or symbolisms to be found in the study of the Feasts was discovered by the late, great Zola Levitt, a Messianic Jewish Scholar who authored many books on our Jewish roots. His son, Mark, who is now Executive Director of Zola Levitt Ministries, graciously allowed me to use an entire chapter from one of Zola's books, "The Seven Feasts of Israel," which explains this discovery. He explains it much better than I could. Here is Chapter 2 from Zola's book:

## II

## UNTO US A CHILD IS BORN

### By Zola Levitt

**A most intriguing and almost startling application of the system of the seven feasts came my way recently during some research for a book. Perhaps this whimsical little section will serve as an example of how God's formulas pervade this earthly, human life.**

I was asked by one of my publishers to look into writing a book about the birth of a baby from a Biblical perspective. The book was to be a gift book to be presented to Christian couples at arrival of blessed events.

This pleasant assignment led me to the many fascinating birth stories in the Bible, including, of course, the wondrous birth of our Lord. But I preferred to do more than just celebrate a new arrival; there are many adequate books for such purposes. Rather I wanted to find some theological principle, perhaps some hidden truth in the Scriptures, about how each of us are born. I wanted to know if the Scriptures held some secret as to how God makes us.

To that end I contacted Dr. Margaret Matheson, a Bible reading friend, and a very good obstetrician who has delivered over ten thousand babies.

I questioned Margaret about pregnancy in general, how it is calculated, and how the baby develops within the mother. I learned that the average pregnancy is 280 days and is counted from the first day of the last menstrual cycle before conception. Making calculations on the Jewish calendar is rather a hobby of mine, and I placed this 280 days on an "ideal Jewish year." The ideal Jewish year would start exactly at the spring equinox, with the first day of Nisan, the new moon of the first month, occurring on the first day of spring, March 21st. Interesting, I found that a pregnancy of 280 days, begun on March 21, would end on a very interesting date, December 25. We don't know if Christmas Day was actually the date of the birth of our Lord, but we do know that Kislev is the accurate date of Chanukah, the Feast of Dedication, which our Lord did commemorate (John 10:22). That discovery led me to think that there must be something very Biblical indeed about the pregnancy term, and I asked Margaret for more details.

It was really Margaret's first statement that turned me on to the whole system I'm about to disclose. I asked Margaret to tell me in some detail just how the baby is made and how it grows, and she began with this statement: "On the fourteenth day of the first month, the egg appears." I couldn't help hearing that familiar ring of Lev. 23:5: *"In the fourteenth day of the first month..."* God's original instruction for the observance of Passover. The Jews use an egg on the Passover table as symbolic of the new life they were granted by the sacrifice of the lamb in Egypt. The egg, of course, appears in the Easter celebration as well, symbolic of the same thing, although not from Biblical sources, as we have seen. The egg is an appropriate enough man-made symbol of a new life, and I was fascinated that the fourteenth day of a pregnancy does the same thing as the fourteenth day of God's festival year: It brings the chance of new life.

I was already thinking in my mind that the baby must develop along the schedule of the seven feasts, but I concealed my excitement from Margaret. I didn't want to encourage her to slant the facts in any way, just to prove a Biblical point. I questioned her carefully, keeping in mind that the next feast, Unleavened Bread, must occur the very next night, the fifteenth day of the first month, according to Lev. 23: 6. I asked Margaret how soon fertilization of the mother's egg must occur if pregnancy is to happen.

Her answer was very clear and very definite. "Fertilization must occur within twenty-four hours or the egg will pass on."

Now I was getting excited. Not only did the two momentous prenatal events occur on the right days, but they were also the appropriate events. The egg, of course, for Passover, and the idea of fertilization - the planting of the seed - for Unleavened Bread, the burial of our Lord. His crucifixion on Passover gave each of us the chance for life everlasting. His burial in the earth, prepared for each of us, the glorious resurrection to come.

I almost held my breath as I inquired about First Fruits. I realized that this third feast is not on a definite time cycle. It simply occurs on the Sunday during the week of Unleavened Bread. It could be the day after, or it could be almost a week away. I asked Margaret cautiously what happened next in the birth process.

"Well, that's a little bit indeterminate," she said. "The fertilized egg travels down the tube at its own speed toward the uterus. It may take anywhere from two to six days before it implants."

I loved her word "implants" because it so suggested the festival of First Fruits, the spring planting, and it was the correct technical term, I found out. The medical term is "implantation." This marks the moment when the fertilized egg arrives safely in the uterus and begins its miraculous growth into a human being.

Needless to say, Margaret and I were very soon occupied with a pile of obstetrical textbooks, embryonic charts, and, of course, the Scriptures in several translations. I appealed to her to help me track this thing down, but I still did not disclose to her just what I was after. I was only going to ask her about how our little fertilized egg would develop, without telling her that I fully expected a very exact schedule in accordance with the feasts.

It's probably not necessary for me to say that I was holding my breath by this time, in hopes that something had really been uncovered. After all, it was so beautiful so far. Surely God designed the conception of each of us in accordance with those first three majestic feasts, so appropriately fulfilled by our Lord.

But would the system continue? The next one was the tough one. It seemed that things were happening fast on the pregnancy schedule, but the seven feasts' schedule now called for that long wait until Pentecost. I asked Margaret cautiously what the next development would be with our implanted egg.

"Well, of course, we have a slowly developing embryo here for a long time," she said. "It goes through stages, but there's really no dramatic change until it becomes an actual fetus. That's the next big event. You can see it all right here on the chart." And she turned her medical book toward me so that I could see a page divided like a calendar, showing the first few weeks of the embryonic development.

I looked across the little pictures at what seemed like a little tadpole, which soon had flippers, and then began to look like a little man from Mars, and so on down to the very last picture on the page. There I saw a human baby, and beside that drawing, the very scriptural message, "Fifty days."

I looked up at Margaret, trying to conceal my excitement, and said carefully, "Is the fiftieth day important?"

"Well," said the obstetrician, "Up until the fiftieth day you wouldn't know if you're going to have a duck or a cocker spaniel. But at the fiftieth day of the embryo, it becomes a human fetus."

Scriptural phrases were flying through my head. "A new creature" seemed to be the appropriate one for the momentous event of the change from this indiscriminate life form, the embryo, to what was essentially a human being. Indeed, on that day of Pentecost, those as yet unregenerate Israelites at the Temple became truly "new creatures". They became spiritual. They received life eternal. They were not the same now as they were before (II Corinthians 5: 17). They would now go on to another life outside the confines of the fleshy bodies they were in, in the manner that that fetus would go on to another life outside the body of its mother.

Margaret apprised me that every scheduled event in the birth of the baby varied somewhat with the particular case, just as the length of the entire pregnancy would vary from mother to mother. The medical book chart had measured its fifty days from fertilization, rather than from implantation (First Fruits in the Scriptures), but the variations among pregnancies would account for the difference. Substantially, after the seventh week, following conception, this embryo - this inhuman life form - would become that one creature created in God's own image.

I next asked Margaret about the first day of the seventh month. I had hoped that there were no big events through what would be the long summer on the schedule of the feasts, and indeed, there were none. It seemed that the fetus, once started on its growth into a human being ready to be born, progressed in a rather general way with nothing momentous happening. The baby, I now realized, had developed very early and now was only gaining size and strength. But, of course, there were a few small perfections to be added by the hand of the Creator, and I was delighted to find that one of these coincided so exactly with the next feast.

The perfection that arrived just at the beginning of the seventh month was the baby's hearing. Margaret's medical textbooks, including the definitive *Williams Obstetrics*, stated that the baby's hearing was now fully developed. At the first day of the seventh month, the baby could discriminate a sound for what it really was. For example, a trumpet was a trumpet! Just in time for the Lord to descend from heaven with a shout and with the sound of the trump of God, that baby could perceive the sounds!

I was now out for blood - that is, the blood that would represent the sixth feast, the Day of Atonement. This was the outstanding day of blood sacrifice, and I specified to Margaret that I wanted to know if there was any development just ten days into the seventh month. I still was careful not to imply just what I was looking for. If Margaret had said, "The elbows are finished," then I suppose my system would have been finished. But somehow I was very confident by now, and the obstetrician didn't let me down.

Half quoting from her textbook and concentrating hard, Margaret stated that the important changes now indeed were in the blood. It was necessary for the fetal blood, which carried the mother's oxygen through the baby's system, to change in such a way that the baby could carry the oxygen that it, itself, would obtain upon birth. Technically, the hemoglobin of the blood would have to change from that of the fetus to that of a self-respirating and circulating human being. The fetus does not breathe, but rather depends on the oxygen obtained through the mother's blood circulation. Naturally, this system must be changed before birth, and that change occurred, according to Margaret's textbooks, in the second week of the seventh month, and to be precise, on the tenth day!

"The blood acceptable" rang through my mind. *"I have given you the blood for remission of sin"* (Leviticus 17:11), was God's statement. Indeed, each person of Israel had to present blood to the Lord through the high priest of Israel on the Day of Atonement. If that blood was acceptable, then there would be life. Likewise, in the fetus, when that blood was mature, there would be life.

But, of course, the fetus is not ready to be born. There remained still another feast, and by this time I was quite confident that Margaret would come up with the appropriate fulfillment. I asked for the fifteenth day of the seventh month, and she immediately recognized the date as the beginning of the safe delivery period.

"You see, that's when the lungs are developed," she said, "And as long as they get their little lungs going, we can bring them along, even if they are born at that early time. I'm afraid if they decide to come before those lungs are finished, then they have very little chance. But by the fifteenth day of the seventh month, a normal baby has two healthy lungs, and if born at that point, can take in its own air and live on it."

The Feast of Tabernacles, I pondered, but, of course, the Tabernacle is the house of the spirit, the spirit is the air in the Bible! Didn't God blow breath into Adam to make him live? Didn't Christ breathe the Holy Spirit upon His disciples? And even more so, in Ezekiel's dry bones vision, (Ezekiel 37) Ezekiel saw God make dead bones, sinews, and muscles come together into human beings, and then commanded the prophet:

> *Then said he unto me, Prophesy unto the wind, prophesy, son of man, and say to the wind, Thus saith the Lord God; Come from four winds, O breath, and breathe upon these slain, that they may live.*
>
> (Ezekiel 37:9)

Tabernacles is the end of the road - the end of the feasts, the end of God's plan, the beginning of the kingdom. The baby would live if born at Tabernacles. The believer will live once he enters the kingdom.

## THE ETERNAL LIGHT

I followed this system still further, even though I had seen in God's feasts on Mt. Sinai, the birth of each one of us. There is still the full 280-day period to consider, which leads to the actual normal birth time. I now had such confidence in the logic of the Bible, that I took out my Jewish calendar again and worked with the added Festival of Dedication, Chanukah. It was not given by God on Mount Sinai, but was prophesied by Daniel (Daniel 8:9-14), and took place in 165 B.C. when the Temple was rededicated.

The nature of Chanukah has to do with the eternal light in the Temple (and in every synagogue today). God had made a great miracle on the occasion when Antiochus entered the Temple and sacrificed a sow on the altar. The Maccabeus threw him out but found only one precious can of consecrated oil - a day's supply - with which to maintain the eternal light. A great miracle answered their prayers, however. The oil lasted eight days and sustained the light until more was ready. And so the Jews still light a candle each night for eight nights on the Feast of Chanukah.

I found what I fully expected on the Jewish calendar. Chanukah lies just the right distance beyond Tabernacles to account for the actual birth of the baby. The 280 days, it occurred to me while working with the Jewish calendar, expressed exactly ten of those mysterious twenty-eight day cycles of the moon, a system more in keeping with the way God would plan things than our Western nine-month pregnancy estimate. In any case, the eight day period of Chanukah accounted for even the off-schedule births, for the most part, and this added festival clearly left a great symbol to the whole system.

Beyond Tabernacles - beyond the Kingdom - we have eternity with God. This then is the fulfillment of the eternal light.

# THE BIRTH OF A KING

All of the above conclusions are given just as I found them out, researching with a friend, the obstetrician. No attempt has been made in a book of this space to create precision medical charts on technical calendars and so forth. I hope to leave that to more scientific minds that could do it justice. But I doubt if a flaw would be found, since we are dealing here with God's Word, and that is the first important point about this interesting discovery.

It shows that the Bible is not just somebody's poetry or somebody's mythology. We don't have to shrink back, defensively claiming that we just "believe" in the Word on something like this. I watched with deep respect as the doctor carefully copied the dates of the seven feasts from the book of Leviticus into her own obstetrical textbooks, so that she might more carefully follow the pregnancies of her patients in the future. I saw that she totally believed some things she had not seen before in all of the time that she had monitored all of those pregnancies. I saw that what God said on Mount Sinai is effective today, useful in a scientific way. More than that, I also saw that each of us has fulfilled the seven feasts in a unique way, before we were actually born! Certainly, each of us developed along the schedule of the feasts, as explained above. In the theory of evolution, it is taught that the embryo and fetus describe some series of past development through other species, which finally produced the human being. But Margaret put into plain words that the explanation of the seven feasts was much better, and the other thing never appealed to her scientifically, in any case. Rather, we can see the Creator, efficient as He is, using certain structures from organism to organism, and with His master-piece, Man, using this magnificent calendar of festi-val occasions and prophetic fulfillments, in the assembly and development of each of these special creatures. Whether we know the feasts or not, we each accomplished every one of them!

And finally, in a great and cosmic way, we are watching Jesus "being born" as King. We saw Him born on earth as the Lamb of God, and His life was quickly snuffed out, but not before His grand pur-pose was accomplished. But in a greater way, we are to see Him come as King when the great Feast of Tabernacles arrives for all of the believers. Thus we have seen our Lord progress through Passover, Unleavened Bread, First Fruits and Pentecost. We shall see Him, soon we pray, in that Feast of Trum-pets, and we shall return with Him on the day of Atonement. But His complete birth cycle, as it were, will see Him crowned as the rightful King of this creation, when that final Tabernacles is reached.

Each of us will then begin that magnificent life with God that we are promised, and our Lord will begin the kingly reign He has so patiently fore-stalled while we work in His fields.

## GOD'S WILL

I thought all of the above would make a superb book, but surprisingly, the publisher turned it down. It had taken a long time to amass the material and present it in book publisher form and the company's interest had moved elsewhere. I tried it on a second and third publisher, with little effect.

I was confused by this. Why would God close a door through which so much light had come? I finally concluded that I would write the material as I have here, in one of these little study guides which I produce myself. However, as the year of 1978 went on, I kept putting off the task.

I kept feeling God's hints and proddings right along. Wasn't this one of those "perfect years" when Chanukah and Christmas arrived together? Would-n't this be a fitting year for this book? But I stood around like the reluctant Gideon, seemingly wait-ing for more of a sign. Finally, God let me have it, and in His typically appropriate way.

My wife became pregnant!

God's will is God's will. I have finally sat down to write! And Baby Boy or Girl Levitt will arrive, if that is God's will, in February of 1979. And if I said these words very close to his secure home in his mother's tummy, he would hear them, I know, because he has just passed his first Feast of Trumpets. Next week God will change my baby's blood and make it acceptable, and the week after that, He will provide him those tabernacles of the Spirit, the lungs.

May we all hear our Father's voice, as he discloses to us, the things that are His in His Word. "

| JEWISH FEAST | CHRISTIAN FULFILLMENT | DEVELOPMENT OF A BABY |
|---|---|---|
| PASSOVER | New Life (Egg) | Ovulation |
| UNLEAVENED BREAD | The Seed | Fertilization |
| FIRST FRUITS | Resurrection | Implantation |
| PENTECOST | Harvest | New Creature (Fetus) |
| TRUMPETS | Rapture | Hearing |
| ATONEMENT | Redemption | Blood (Hemoglobin A) |
| TABERNACLES | Kingdom | Lungs |
| CHANUKAH | Eternity | Eternal Life |

39

**77**

# CHART 1

## THE JEWS 2 CALENDARS COMPARED TO OURS

## SECULAR YEAR BEGINS TISHRI 1.

## RELIGIOUS YEAR BEGINS NISAN 1.

# CHART 2

## THE 2 JEWISH CALENDARS

RELIGIOUS                    SECULAR OR CIVIL

1. Nisan or Abib (Canaanite)        1. Tishri or Ethanim
2. Iyyar or Ziv (Canaanite)         2. Marcheshvan or Bul
3. Sivan                            3. Chislev
4. Tammuz                           4. Tebeth
5. Ab                               5. Shebat
6. Eul                              6. Adar
7. Tishri or Ethanim (Canaanite)    7. Nisan or Abib
8. Marcheshvan or Bul (Canaanite)   8. Iyyar or Ziv
9. Chislev                          9. Sivan
10. Tebeth                          10. Tammuz
11. Shebat                          11. Ab
12. Adar                            12. Eul

### SECULAR CALENDAR BEGAN WITH ADAM

**Genesis 7:11** *In the six hundredth year of Noah's life, in the second month, the seventeenth day of the month, the same day were all the fountains of the great deep broken up, and the windows of heaven were opened.*

**Genesis 8:5** *And the waters decreased continually until the tenth month. In the tenth month, on the first day of the month, the tops of the mountains were seen.*

**Genesis 8:4** *And the ark rested in the seventh month, on the seventeenth day of the month, upon the mountains of Ararat.*

### RELIGIOUS CALENDAR BEGAN
### WITH THE FIRST PASSOVER

**Exodus 12:2** *This month shall be unto you the beginning of months: it shall be the first month of the year to you.*

**Exodus 13:4** *This day came ye out in the month Abib.*

**79**

# CHAPTER THREE ENDNOTES

39.   The Seven Feasts of Israel by Zola Levitt. © 1979. Reprinted with permission from Zola Levitt Ministries www.levitt.com.

# CHAPTER FOUR

## THE AMAZING PRECISION OF GOD IN THE FULFILLING OF THE SPRING FEASTS

Let's suppose for just a moment that you or I were separated from our loved ones for an extended period of time much like some of our military is at the present time. Let's also suppose that during this period of separation, one of our loved ones had a birthday, anniversary or some other event that we knew about. Wouldn't it mean a great deal to that loved one to receive a phone call, a card or some other sort of acknowledgement from you to let them know you loved them and were thinking about them even though you were separated? Of course it would.

I think I can see that same scenario playing out in the way God has caused and is causing events to happen exactly on feast days. He loves us all but especially His "Chosen People" and is reminding us all that He's still there, still in control, still loves us, and is still working out His plan for us. Critics may call it a coincidence that the events happened on feast days, but when other important events in God's work with man keep happening on anniversaries of feast days, it gets harder and harder to explain as a coincidence. The Jewish Rabbis say that "coincidence" is not a "Kosher" word in dealing with God's work.[40]

Let's begin with the first feast of Passover and identify some of the dates of other events that happened on the exact anniversary of this feast day. Passover is the first of the 3 Spring Feasts that all happen concurrently. All 3 of these feasts are lumped together and commonly referred to today as "Passover" and last for 8 days. You frequently hear the term, "Passover Week" referring to the feasts of Passover, Unleavened Bread and First-fruits. The Old Testament, however, breaks each one down separately and refers to it separately so first of all, let's pin down the date of Passover exactly from Leviticus 23 and look at some of the actions performed in the observance of this feast.

## FEAST 1 OF THE SPRING FEASTS: PASSOVER OR PESACH

### *Leviticus 23:5:*

*In the fourteenth day of the first month at evening is the LORD'S Passover.*

### ACTIONS

● **Eat Seder or Passover meal.**

● **Tell children the story of Passover. "Why is this night different from all others?"**

● **Passover is one day in length but in Jesus' time was celebrated on either the night of the**

**14th or the 15th. The Seder or Passover Meal was celebrated on either night. Jesus and his disciples ate the Seder probably on the 14th and the priests did not eat theirs until the 15th. See John 18:28.**

- **It is not a "Sabbath" unless it falls on a Saturday. Work and travel is permitted.**

Note that this feast day is determined by the $14^{th}$ day of the month. This means that through the years it can occur on any day of the week. Some of the other feasts will occur only on specific days of the week but this feast and the feast of Unleavened Bread that follows it on the next day, are determined by the day of the month and can occur on any day of the week. The first month on the Jewish "Religious" calendar is Nisan and it occurs in our months of March or April depending on the year. There are 2 calendars in use in the Jewish culture today: a religious calendar and a secular calendar. The "religious" calendar is used to determine all of the 7 Feast days. We will explain the difference in the 2 calendars a little later in this chapter.

As I begin to list the events that took place on the dates of these feasts, some of the dates are provable by scripture, some are provable by Jewish literature outside of our present Old and New Testaments and some of them are just likely but not provable by present day documents. I have used extensive footnotes in this study so don't just take my word for it. Research it yourself. Remember the Bereans.

*These were more noble than those in Thessalonica, in that they received the word with all readi-*

*ness of mind, and searched the scriptures daily, whether those things were so.*

(Acts 17:11 AV)

### Events that occurred on the 14ᵗʰ of Nisan:

● The Jews killed the Passover lamb and ate the first Passover meal. They applied the blood of the Lamb over the doorposts of their houses and were protected from the death of the firstborn decreed by God on that night.[41]

● The "Religious Calendar" was created. God told them:

*This month [shall be] unto you the beginning of months: it [shall be] the first month of the year to you.*

(Exodus 12:2 AV)

*And this day shall be unto you for a memorial; and ye shall keep it a feast to the LORD throughout your generations; ye shall keep it a feast by an ordinance for ever.*

(Exodus 12:14 AV)

The first Passover took place in the 7ᵗʰ month (Abib or Nisan) of the Jewish calendar.[42] From that time on, the 7ᵗʰ month became the 1ˢᵗ month. The names of the months remained basically the same, but the beginning of the year was moved from the 7ᵗʰ month to the 1ˢᵗ month. It appears all dates in the Old and New Testaments after this time are based on this "Religious Calendar".[43]

Jewish culture also retained the old calendar or "Secular Calendar" and it is used as well as the "Religious Calendar" today.

- **Fulfillment:** Jesus (Yeshua to the Messianic Jews) was crucified. He died at the 9th hour or about 3PM at the time when the Passover lambs were to be slain.

**"In Mark 14:12, it is written, "And the first day of unleavened bread, when they killed the Passover [the *Pesach* lamb] ...." The word translated as first is the Greek word *protos,* which means "before, earlier, and preceding." Because there was a temple *(Beit HaMikdash)* in Jerusalem *(Yerushalayim)* in the days of *Yeshua,* the First Seder would be on the fourteenth of Nisan, and the Second Seder on the fifteenth. The Seder could be held on either night. *Yeshua* had His Passover *(Pesach)* Seder by midnight on the fourteenth of Nisan (remember that the fourteenth of Nisan begins at sundown, which is roughly six hours prior to midnight), and was crucified the next afternoon at 3:00 p.m., which is still the fourteenth of Nisan."[44]**

In Jesus time, some 1500 years after Passover was set up in Exodus 12, the population had grown until the priests could no longer slaughter all the lambs in one day.[45] They decreed that the Passover Seder could be observed on either the 14th or the 15th. There is evidence of this practice in John 18:28.

> *Then led they Jesus from Caiaphas unto the hall of judgment: and it was early; and they themselves went not into the judgment hall, lest they should be defiled; but that they might eat the Passover.*
>
> (John 18:28 AV)

Jesus had eaten His Passover Seder on the night before and the priests had not yet eaten theirs.

● Passover becomes Communion.

*And he took bread, and gave thanks, and brake [it], and gave unto them, saying, This is my body which is given for you: this do in remembrance of me.*

(Luke 22:19 AV)

● John the Baptist born on Passover? This is one of those events that is likely but not provable.

The reasoning goes like this: In Luke 1:5 is the story of how John's father, Zacharias, was visited by the angel Gabriel and was told he and his wife Elizabeth would have a son. Zacharias was one of the priests serving at the temple. In those days the temple duty was divided up into groups or courses. We are told in Luke 1:5 that Zacharias is of the course of Abia. We can turn back to 1 Chronicles 24:10 and learn that the course of Abia was the eighth group of priests to serve. There were 24 courses of priests and each served two regular 1 week shifts at different times of the year. In addition to the 1 week shifts, all the priests from all the courses served in the Temple on the feast days when all the people were required to come to Jerusalem. These feasts were: Unleavened Bread, Pentecost/Feast of Weeks, and Tabernacles and are known as the "Pilgrim Feasts."[46] By putting all this information together, and counting off his weeks of service, one can determine that Zacharias left the Temple and went home to Elizabeth on or about the first week of the Jewish month of Sivan or the last week in May by our calendar. Allowing 2 weeks for the laws of separation God commanded in Leviticus 12:5, 15:19, 24-25 for the conception, the birth date of John the Baptist would have been close to Passover of the following year.

To further add to the belief that John was born on Passover, Jesus said in Matthew 11:

*For all the prophets and the law prophesied until John. And if ye will receive it, this is Elias, which was for to come. He that hath ears to hear, let him hear.*

(Matthew 11:13-15 AV)

Also in Matthew 17:

*And his disciples asked him, saying, Why then say the scribes that Elias must first come? And Jesus answered and said unto them, Elias truly shall first come, and restore all things. But I say unto you, that Elias is come already, and they knew him not, but have done unto him whatsoever they listed. Likewise shall also the Son of man suffer of them. Then the disciples understood that he spake unto them of John the Baptist.*

(Matthew 17:10-13 AV)

The end of the Old Testament says:

*Behold, I will send you Elijah the prophet before the coming of the great and dreadful day of the LORD:*

(Malachi 4:5 AV)

The angel Gabriel told Zacharias, John's father, these things about the son to be born to him:

**89**

*For he shall be great in the sight of the Lord, and shall drink neither wine nor strong drink; and he shall be filled with the Holy Ghost, even from his mother's womb.  And many of the children of Israel shall he turn to the Lord their God.  And he shall go before him **in the spirit and power of Elias**, to turn the hearts of the fathers to the children, and the disobedient to the wisdom of the just; to make ready a people prepared for the Lord.*

(Luke 1:15-17, emphasis added)

Jewish tradition said that Elijah would come at Passover and to this day the Jews set a cup for Elijah and leave the door open so he can enter when they observe Passover.  If John the Baptist was born on Passover, he would have fulfilled the coming of the "Spirit and Power of Elijah" as Jesus said.

We know that Christmas is likely not the real birthday of Jesus. Evidence points to the fact that He was born in the early fall.  If Passover really was the birthdate of John the Baptist, then let's look at Luke 1:26-27:

*And in the sixth month the angel Gabriel was sent from God unto a city of Galilee, named Nazareth, To a virgen espoused to a man whose name was joseph, of the house of David and the virgin's name was Mary.*

That would mean that Jesus was born 6 months after John's birth on Passover and His birth would be just about the time of the Fall Feasts.  These 3 feasts occur within a 15 day period of time and Jesus could have been born on any of the three dates with Rosh Hashanah/Feast of Trum-

**90**

pets being the most likely in my opinion. Several other writers I have studied also make a good case for Jesus being born on the Feast of Tabernacles or even Yom Kippur, the Day of Atonement. One of the most fascinating concepts of the fact that Jesus was born on one of the fall feasts days is that when you count back 280 days, (the average human conception period) the date of conception figures very close to the 25th of the Jewish month of Kislev. This is the Jewish feast of Hanukkah at about our Christmas time. Could it be that instead of celebrating the birth of Jesus at Christmas, we are really celebrating His Conception? After all, that was the real miracle. Many babies have been born but only one was ever conceived in a virgin by the Holy Spirit.

John being born on one feast day and Jesus being born on another would fit the pattern emerging from our study of the feasts. I'd like to tell you that these dates were the real birthdates of both Jesus and John the Baptist but I can't. We have just enough information to know it's likely, but not enough to say it's true.

# FEAST 2 OF THE SPRING FEASTS
## Unleavened Bread/Hag HaMatzah/Matzot.
### *Leviticus 23:6-8:*

*And on the fifteenth day of the same month is the feast of unleavened bread unto the LORD: seven days ye must eat unleavened bread. In the first day ye shall have an holy convocation: ye shall do no servile work therein. But ye shall offer an offering made by fire unto the LORD seven days:*

**91**

*in the seventh day is an holy convocation: ye shall do no servile work therein.*

## Pilgrim Feast.

### *Deuteronomy 16:16-17:*

*Three times in a year shall all thy males appear before the LORD thy God in the place which he shall choose; in the feast of unleavened bread, and in the feast of weeks, and in the feast of tabernacles: and they shall not appear before the LORD empty: Every man shall give as he is able, according to the blessing of the LORD thy God which he hath given thee. {as...: Heb. according to the gift of his hand)*

(A) Feast lasts 7 days
(B) High Holy Day (Shabbaton) on first day.
(C) High Holy Day (Shabbaton) on seventh day.
(D) Requires the presence of every able-bodied male in Jerusalem.
(E) They shall not come empty-handed.

## ACTIONS

- Purge house of leaven.
- Eat no leaven.
- Make a daily sacrifice.
- Observe first and last days as Sabbaths. (No work and limited travel. Travel was limited to 800-900 yards or 2,000 cubits. )

The second of the 3 concurrent and intertwined spring feasts is the Feast of Unleavened Bread. Notice it begins on the 15th of the Jewish month of Nisan, which means the first day of the feast can and does occur on any day of the week. Both the first and the last day of this 7 day feast are "High Holy Days" and are treated just like the weekly Sabbath Day that occurs every Saturday. It is possible and likely to have three "Sabbath Days" during the week of Unleavened Bread. There will always be two. Why am I making a point of explaining this?

Was Jesus crucified on a Friday? This one thing causes and has caused much confusion in the Body of Christ. In the early days of what later came to be known as the Roman Catholic Church, around 300 to 400 AD., the church leaders were very anti-Semitic and did not make any detailed study of Jewish culture. They ruled that Jesus was crucified on a Friday because the New Testament writers said it was the day before the Sabbath which they interpreted as being the Saturday Sabbath. The New Testament states:

> *Now the Feast of Unleavened Bread drew near, which is called Passover.*
>
> (Luke 22:1)

> *And now when the even was come, because it was the preparation, that is, the day before the Sabbath.*
>
> (Mark 16:42)

> *This man went unto Pilate, and begged the body of Jesus. And he took it down, and wrapped it in linen, and laid it in a sepulcher that was hewn in stone, wherein never man before was laid. And*

*that day was the preparation, and the Sabbath drew on.*

(Luke 23:52-54)

If the Sabbath referred to in these scriptures is referring to the regular weekly Sabbath (Saturday) then Jesus was indeed crucified on a Friday. I believe, however, the Sabbath referred to was the first day of Unleavened Bread. It is always treated as a Sabbath no matter on what day of the week it occurs. If these scriptures do refer to the first day of Unleavened Bread and not a Saturday Sabbath, Jesus could have been crucified on another day of the week.

Jesus said in Matthew 12:40, emphasis mine:

*For as Jonah was **three days and three nights** in the belly of the great fish, so will the Son of Man be **three days and three nights** in the heart of the earth.*

The explanation which the proponents of a Friday crucifixion give is that each part of a day is counted as a day. Even using that reasoning as an explanation, it is not possible to count 3 days **and** 3 nights in the period between Friday afternoon and Sunday morning when the women found the tomb empty. Who do you believe? The early leaders of the Roman Catholic Church who said He was crucified on Friday or Jesus Himself who said He would be 3 days **and** 3 nights in the heart of the earth? I choose to believe what Jesus said. Nowhere in the New Testament does it say He was crucified on Friday. It does say His tomb was found empty on the first day of the week which is Sunday. Jesus said He would be 3 days and 3 nights in the heart of the earth. If you count back 3 days and 3 nights from Sunday morning, a crucifixion on Wednesday would seem logical.

Here is the way I think it happened. Jesus was crucified on a Wednesday. Since it was Passover at exactly the time the lambs were killed at the hour that He died, we know it was the 14th of the Jewish month of Nisan. He was put in the tomb in the late afternoon hours of Wednesday the 14th. It had to be before about 6PM because about 6PM or twilight, marked the beginning of a new day. The new day that began that twilight was Thursday, the 15th of Nisan, and was the first day of the Feast of Unleavened Bread and a "High Holy Day" in which no work could be done just like the Saturday Sabbath.

Jesus lay in the tomb during the daytime and nighttime hours of Thursday, Friday and Saturday to fulfill the 3 days **and** 3 nights in the heart of the earth and arose in either the closing hours of Saturday or the beginning hours of Sunday. The tomb was found empty after daylight on Sunday. The ladies who found the tomb empty would have been unable to travel or work on Thursday because it was a Sabbath. On Friday, however, they probably collected the spices they brought with them on Sunday morning.[47] After collecting the spices on Friday, they would have had to stay home on Saturday, because it also was a Sabbath. When the Sabbaths were past, they went to the tomb on Sunday morning.[48] None of this could be understood without an understanding of the feast days and the fact that **the day after Passover is _always_ a Sabbath no matter on which day of the week it falls.**

Unleavened Bread is a "Pilgrim Feast" and requires the presence of every able-bodied male in Jerusalem. Each one must bring a sacrifice or offering.

*Three times in a year shall all thy males appear before the LORD thy God in the place which he shall choose; in the feast of unleavened bread, and in the feast of weeks, and in the feast of tabernacles: and they shall not appear before the LORD empty.*

(Deuteronomy 16:16 AV)

*Every man [shall give] as he is able, according to the blessing of the LORD thy God which he hath given thee.*

(Deuteronomy 16:17 AV)

Because of these 3 feasts requiring the presence of every able-bodied male in Jerusalem, the city was always packed during these feast times. Every guest room was full and all the hotels and inns were full to overflowing. If you travel to Jerusalem today during one of these 3 feasts, the same is true.

Besides the sacrifices and offerings required, there were several other actions that must be taken during the Feast of Unleavened Bread.

In the days before the feast, the family of each house made a thorough search of the house and removed anything that had leaven. After a thorough and ceremonious search, the father took a feather and a wooden spoon and symbolically swept the last crumbs of leaven, whether real or imaginary, into a wooden spoon. On the day before the

**96**

feast, the 14th of Nisan, the father wraps the feather, spoon and leaven in a linen cloth and takes it to the temple where it is thrown into a fire to be burned.

## FULFILLMENT:

Leaven is symbolic of sin. The wooden spoon is symbolic of the tree Jesus died upon.[49] Sweeping the leaven onto the spoon is symbolic of Jesus taking our sins onto Himself on the cross.[50] Jesus was then wrapped in linen and cast out of His house (His Body) and went to hell which is a place of burning.[51] His body, wrapped in linen, lay in the tomb during the first few days of this feast.[52]

**Events That Occurred During the Week of Unleavened Bread Beginning on the 15th of Nisan and Lasting 7 Days.**

- Jesus' body lay in the tomb during the first few days of the week. He arose on the third day after Passover (Nisan 17), and appeared to His disciples and others during the week.

- Moses led the nation of Israel out of Egypt and bondage "on the morrow" after the first Passover meal or Seder.

*And Moses wrote their goings out according to their journeys by the commandment of the LORD: and these [are] their journeys according to their goings out. And they departed from Rameses in the first month, on the fifteenth day of the first month; on the morrow after the Passover the chil-*

**97**

*dren of Israel went out with an high hand in the sight of all the Egyptians.*
>                    (Numbers 33:2-3 AV)

● Jacob led his family into Egypt to save them from the famine in the land on the exact anniversary in advance of the day Moses led them out.  They stayed and multiplied to become a nation led out of bondage by Moses 430 years later.

*And it came to pass at the end of the four hundred and thirty years, <u>even the selfsame day it came to pass</u>, that all the hosts of the LORD went out from the land of Egypt.*
>                    (Exodus 12:41 AV, emphasis mine)

● Water of Marah made sweet when the Lord showed Moses a tree to cast into the water.  This occurred 6 days after their departure from Ramses on the fifteenth.  It would have been the next to last day of the Feast of Unleavened Bread or Nisan 21.[53]

● All the events of Firstfruits listed with the next feast occurred this week also since Firstfruits occurs during the week of Unleavened Bread.

## FEAST 3 OF THE SPRING FEASTS

### First Fruits or Bikkurim.

*Speak unto the children of Israel, and say unto them, When ye be come into the land which I give unto you, and shall reap the harvest thereof, then ye shall bring a sheaf of the firstfruits of your harvest unto the priest: (sheaf or, handful: Heb.*

**98**

*omer) And he shall wave the sheaf before the LORD, to be accepted for you: on the morrow after the Sabbath the priest shall wave it. And ye shall offer that day when ye wave the sheaf and the lamb without blemish of the first year for a burnt offering unto the LORD.*

(Lev. 23: 10-12)

1. The Sabbath in verse 11 is the 7th day, Saturday Sabbath (Shabbot) that occurs after the High Holy Day (Shabbaton) that is the first day of Unleavened Bread.

2. It is "on the morrow" after the Sabbath (Saturday) so it always occurs on Sunday.

3. It also always occurs during the 7 days of the Feast of Unleavened Bread.

4. It occurs 2 to 6 days after Passover.

## ACTIONS

- **Already in Jerusalem.**
- **Priests wave sheaf offering. (Firstfruits)**
- **Priests offer lamb of the first year as burnt offering.**
- **Priests offer bread offering.**
- **Priests offer wine offering.**
- **Work and travel is permitted.**

The third of the 3 concurrent and intertwined spring feasts is the Feast of Firstfruits. It is a one day feast that occurs during the week of the Feast of Unleavened Bread.

It is not determined by the day of the month, but by the day of the week. It occurs on the day after the regular Saturday Sabbath in the week of the Feast of Unleavened Bread. It is always on a Sunday. It will occur from 2 to 6 days after Passover (Nisan 14). It appears to have occurred on the 3rd day after Passover in years when important events occurred. It was traditionally the time when the first of the new crop of grain was gathered and brought as an offering to the Lord.

The Feast of Unleavened Bread is a Pilgrim Feast requiring the presence of every able-bodied male in Jerusalem so since Firstfruits occurs during that week, everyone is on hand for the celebration.

The High Priest would wave the first of the grain harvest before the Lord and offer it to Him as the first of the new crop.

## FULFILLMENT:

Jesus arose sometime in either the closing hours of Saturday or the beginning hours of Sunday (Firstfruits). His tomb was found empty early in the morning on the first day of the week or Sunday (Firstfruits).

Early Sunday morning when Mary saw Jesus:

*Jesus saith unto her, 'Touch me not; for I am not yet ascended to my Father: but go to my brethren, and say unto them, I ascend unto my Father, and your Father; and [to] my God, and your God.'*
(John 20:17 AV)

*But now is Christ risen from the dead, [and] become the firstfruits of them that slept.*
(1 Corinthians 15:20 AV)

Jesus ascended on that Sunday to act as our High Priest and present Himself as the Firstfruits of the new crop of all those who accept Him and are born again by faith in His Death, Burial and Resurrection.

## EVENTS THAT OCCURRED ON THE FEAST DAY OF FIRSTFRUITS

- **Jesus' tomb found empty. He ascended to become the Firstfruits of all who believe. Matthew 28:1, Mark 16:2, Luke 24:1, John 20:1.**

- **Red Sea split.** This is first alluded to in Exodus 5:3:

*And they said, The God of the Hebrews hath met with us: let us go, we pray thee, three days' journey into the desert, and sacrifice unto the LORD our God; lest he fall upon us with pestilence, or with the sword.*
(Exodus 5:3 AV)

Moses' journal of their travels in Numbers 33:2-8 *lists their daily camps.*

Traditional Jewish literature identifies The Feast of Firstfruits as the very day God split the Red Sea and they crossed over.

- **The manna ceased and the Jews ate of the firstfruits of the Promised Land.**

*And they did eat of the old corn of the land on the morrow after the Passover, unleavened cakes, and parched [corn] in the selfsame day. And the manna ceased on the morrow after they had eaten of the old corn of the land; neither had the children of Israel manna any more; but they did eat of the fruit of the land of Canaan that year.*

(Joshua 5:11-12 AV)

The morrow after the Passover would have been the 15th of Nisan when they ate of the old corn. On the next day the manna ceased, which would have been the 16th of Nisan. On the next day, they ate of the firstfruits of the land. **This was the 17th of Nisan and the Feast of Firstfruits 3 days after Passover.**

- **Haman was hanged on his own gallows.**

In the Book of Esther we meet Haman, who is plotting to kill all the Jews and Mordecai in particular. In Esther 3 we find Haman manipulating King Ahasuerus into issuing a decree that all the Jews will be killed on a date later that same year.[54] After Mordecai consulted with Esther, she proclaimed a three day fast which would have been on Nisan 14-16.[55] Esther then came in to King Ahasuerus at the risk of her life on the 16th of Nisan. The King asked Esther what he could do for her. She requested the King and Haman to come on this same day to a banquet she had prepared for them. This was on the 16th of Nisan.

At that banquet, the King again asked Esther what she wanted and Esther requested that the King and Haman come to another banquet the following night. This last banquet would have been on the 17th of Nisan. It is at this last banquet on the night of the 17[56] of Nisan that the King decrees that Haman be hanged on his own gallows.[56]

Jewish tradition recognizes this event as occurring on the Feast of Firstfruits.[57]

- **Noah and his family delivered. Genesis 8:4, Exodus 12:2, Exodus 13:4.**

This one takes just a bit of explaining but stay with me. It is worth it. In Genesis 8, verse 4 we find that:

*And the ark rested in the seventh month, on the seventeenth day of the month, upon the mountains of Ararat.*

Remember the calendar change in Exodus 12:2 at the first Passover? Since then, the new or Religious calendar is the one in use for all dates in Scripture. In Exodus 13:4, we find that the calendar change took place in the 7th month of the old or Secular calendar or the month of Abib. (See calendar chart.) The 7th month of the old or Secular calendar became the 1st month of the new or Religious calendar. The old or Secular calendar was in use in Genesis when the above verse was written. In Jesus' time, the new or Religious calendar was in use. Jesus was crucified on Passover or the 14th of Nisan. He arose on the 17th of Nisan after 3 days and 3 nights. **The day identified in Genesis 8:4 as the day the Ark rested on the mountains of Ararat was the exact anniversary in advance of the day Jesus arose.** How fitting. Noah and his family were delivered from judgment by the ark on the exact anniversary in advance of the day Jesus delivered us from the judgment of sin.

# FEAST 4 AND THE LAST OF THE SPRING FEASTS
## Pentecost/ Shavuot/ Feast of Weeks.

*And ye shall count unto you from the morrow after the Sabbath, from the day that ye brought the sheaf of the wave offering; seven Sabbaths shall be complete: Even unto the morrow after the seventh Sabbath shall ye number fifty days; and ye shall offer a new meat offering unto the LORD.*

(Leviticus 23:15-16)

### Pilgrim Feast

*Three times in a year shall all thy males appear before the LORD thy God in the place which he shall choose; in the feast of unleavened bread, and in the feast of weeks, and in the feast of tabernacles: and they shall not appear before the LORD empty: Every man shall give as he is able, according to the blessing of the LORD thy God which he hath given thee.  (as...: Heb. according to the gift of his hand)*

(Deuteronomy 16: 16-17)

1.  It is "on the morrow" after the seventh Sabbath so it always occurs on Sunday.

2.  It is 50 days after Firstfruits.

3.  Requires the presence of every able-bodied male in Jerusalem.

4.  They shall not come empty-handed.

# ACTIONS

- **Journey to Jerusalem.**

- **Bring offering.**

- **Priests make new grain offering.**

- **Priests make bread offering.**

- **Priests offer 7 lambs, 1 bullock and 2 rams. 1 kid goat for a sin offering and 2 lambs of the first year for a peace offering.**

- **Observe the day of Pentecost as a Sabbath. (No work and limited travel. Travel was limited to 800-900 yards or 2,000 cubits.) Leviticus 23:21**

This last of the Spring Feasts occurs 50 days after First-fruits. Notice the counting from Firstfruits not Passover or Unleavened Bread. **Firstfruits always occurs on a Sunday** and this feast, **Pentecost, also always occurs on a Sunday**. The counting instructions is not to count 50 days as you might suppose, but to count 7 Sabbaths (Saturdays) and the next day will be Pentecost; in other words, 7 times 7 or 49+1.

Pentecost, as well as Unleavened Bread and Tabernacles, is one of the 3 Pilgrim Feasts requiring that every able bodied male journey to Jerusalem for the feast. They must all present an offering. In Acts 2, when the Holy Spirit was given to the church, Acts 2:5 says:

*And there were dwelling at Jerusalem Jews, devout men, out of every nation under heaven.*

**105**

The reason for the large crowds there from many nations was that they had come to Jerusalem to observe the Pilgrim Feast of Pentecost. Deuteronomy 16:16 required them to come to Jerusalem from wherever they were at these 3 feasts. That was part of their worship for every professing Jew. These rules still apply today and Jerusalem is still crowded on these feast days.

The day of Pentecost is also commanded to be regarded as a Sabbath with no work being done and limited travel. As I said before, Pentecost is always on a Sunday and is regarded as a Sabbath. The day before is the regular weekly Sabbath or Saturday. There will always be 2 Sabbaths, one after another at Pentecost; one Saturday Sabbath and one Sunday Sabbath because of the feast day.

## FULFILLMENT

50 days after Jesus arose, the Holy Spirit was given to the Church on Pentecost Sunday as recorded in Acts 2. In the upper room where 120 believers had gathered "in one place and with one accord" tongues of fire came down and a sound as of a mighty rushing wind filled the place. Later, Peter preached and 3000 Jews were saved. God established His Covenant of Grace on that day.

50 days after the parting of the Red Sea, Moses went up the mountain to meet God. God wrote His Laws in the tablets of stone with His Finger and Moses received the tablets. God established his Covenant of Law on the anniversary in advance of the day the Holy Spirit was given in Acts 2.

# CHAPTER FOUR ENDNOTES

40. Chuck Missler-numerous commentaries.

41. Exodus 12

42. Exodus 13:4

43.

*And it came to pass in the four hundred and eight-ieth year after the children of Israel had come out of the land of Egypt, in the fourth year of Solomon's reign over Israel, in the month of Ziv, which is the second month, that he began to build the house of the LORD.*

(1 Kings 6:1)

*And in the eleventh year, in the month of Bul,which is the eighth month, the house was finished in all its details and according to all its plans. So he was seven years in building it.*

(1 Kings 6:38)

44. Materials from "The Seven Festivals of the Messi-ah", by Edward Chumney, copyright 1994, used by permission of Destiny Image Publishers, 167 Walnut BottomRoad, Shippensburg, PA17257 www.destinyimage.com

45. Steven Ger, The Unleavened Messiah Video, Sojurner Ministries
http://www.sojournerministries.com/

46.

*Three times in a year shall all thy males appear before the LORD thy God in the place which he shall choose; in the feast of unleavened bread, and in the feast of weeks, and in the feast of tabernacles: and they shall not appear before the LORD empty:*

(Deuteronomy 16:16 AV)

47. Mark 16:1

48. Matthew 28:1

49.

*And if a man have committed a sin worthy of death, and he be put to death, and thou hang him on a tree.*

(Deuteronomy 21:22 AV)

50.

*For he hath made him [to be] sin for us, who knew no sin; that we might be made the righteousness of God in him.*

(2 Corinthians 5:21 AV)

51.

*Now that he ascended, what is it but that he also descended first into the lower parts of the earth? He that descended is the same also that ascended up far above all heavens, that he might fill all things.*

(Ephesians 4:9-10 AV)

52.

*Then arose Peter, and ran unto the sepulchre;
and stooping down, he beheld the linen clothes
laid by themselves, and departed, wondering in
himself at that which was come to pass.*

(Luke 24:12 AV)

*And the napkin, that was about his head, not
lying with the linen clothes, but wrapped together in a place by itself.*

(John 20:7 AV)

53. Numbers 33:2-8 & Exodus 15:22-25

54. Esther 3:12-13

55. Esther 4:16

56. Esther 7:9-10

57. Edward Chumney. The Seven Festivals of the
Messiah. © 1994, p.62- Destiny Image, Shippenburg,
Pa.

# CHAPTER FIVE

## THE FAST OF TISHA B'AV

In any study of Jewish culture and history, it quickly becomes evident that there are supernatural forces working behind the scenes mightily both for and against God's Chosen People. God is affirming His Word and His Plan for all mankind by the events that have happened and will happen on the Jews Feast Days. There are other events, however, that are occurring on what appears to be another plan and another agenda and they are happening on specific dates just like the events that are occurring on the feast days. I'm not going to tell you I know why they are happening, but they are happening. To my knowledge, these events have nothing to do with our study of the feasts and are significant only because they are occurring on a specific date. Let's take time out from our study of the feasts and let me introduce you to the strange story of Tisha B'Av or the 9th day of the Jewish month of Av. This information is from the internet encyclopedia, Wikipedia:

| Tisha B'Av | |
|---|---|
| **Official name** | Hebrew: באב העשת<br>English: Ninth of Av |
| **Observed by** | Jews in Judaism |
| **Type** | Jewish |
| **Significance** | Mourning for the destruction of the First & Second Temples in Jerusalem |
| **Date** | 9th day of Av |
| **2006 date** | sunset, August 2 – sunset, August 3 |
| **2007 date** | sunset, July 23 – sunset, July 24 |
| **Observances** | Fasting, prayer |
| **Related to** | The fasts of the Tenth of Tevet and the Seventeenth of Tammuz, the Three Weeks & the Nine Days |

**Tisha B'Av** or **Tish'ah b'Av** (Hebrew: באב העשת or באב יט, *tish'āh ba-āḇ*) is a major annual fast day in Judaism. Its name denotes the ninth day (*Tisha*) of the Jewish month of *Av*, which falls in July or August. It has been called the "saddest day in Jewish history".[1]

# BACKGROUND

## The destructions

The fast commemorates two of the saddest events in Jewish history — the destruction of the First Temple (originially built by <u>King Solomon</u>), and the destruction of the Second Temple. Those two events occurred about 656 years apart, but both in the same month, Av, and, as tradition has it, both on the ninth day.

In connection with the fall of Jerusalem, three other fast-days were established at the same time as the Ninth Day of Av: these were the Tenth of Tevet, when the siege began; the Seventeenth of Tammuz, when the first breach was made in the wall; and the Third of Tishrei, known as the <u>Fast of Gedaliah</u>, the day when Gedaliah was assassinated (<u>2 Kings</u> 25:25; <u>Jeremiah</u> 41:2). From <u>Zechariah</u> 7:5, 8:19 it appears that after the building of the Second Temple the custom of keeping these fast-days was temporarily discontinued. Since the destruction of Jerusalem and of the Second Temple by the <u>Romans</u>, the four fast-days have again been observed.

# AFTER THE EXODUS

On this day in the year 1312 BCE, the generation of Jews who came out of Egypt under <u>Moses</u>' leadership 16 months earlier were condemned to die in the wilderness (*midbar*) and the entry into the <u>Land of Israel</u> was delayed for 40 years until the old generation died out.

# THE FIVE CALAMITIES

According to the <u>Mishnah</u> (*Taanit*, 4:6), five specific events occurred on the ninth of Av that warrant fasting:

1. On this day, the <u>twelve spies</u> sent by Moses to observe the land of <u>Canaan</u> returned from their mission. Two of the spies (<u>Joshua</u> and <u>Caleb</u>) brought a positive report, but 10 of the spies brought an "evil report" about the land that caused the <u>Children of Israel</u> to cry, panic and despair of ever entering the "<u>Promised land</u>". For this, they were punished by God that they would not enter, and that for all generations the day would become one of crying and misfortune for the descendants of the Children of Israel, the Jewish people. (See <u>Numbers</u> chapters 13-14)

2. Solomon's Temple (the First Temple) and the <u>Kingdom of Judah</u> were destroyed by the <u>Babylonians</u> led by <u>Nebuchadnezzar</u> in <u>586 BCE</u> and the Judeans were sent into the <u>Babylonian exile</u>.

3. The Second Temple was destroyed by the Roman Empire in <u>70 CE</u> scattering the people of <u>Judea</u> and commencing a two thousand year <u>Jewish exile</u>.

4. The <u>Bar Kokhba's revolt</u> against Rome failed, and <u>Bar Kokhba</u> was killed, as was <u>Rabbi Akiva</u> and many other important <u>sages</u> of the Mishnah, and <u>Betar</u> was destroyed.

5. Following the <u>Siege of Jerusalem</u>, the subsequent razing of <u>Jerusalem</u> occurred one year later.

According to the <u>Talmud</u> (Tractate Taanit), the destruction of the Second Temple began on that date and was finally consumed by the flames on the next day — the Tenth of Av.

## LATER CALAMITIES ON 9 AV

A large number of calamities are alleged to have occurred on the ninth of Av:

- The declaration of the <u>Crusades</u> by <u>Pope Urban II</u> in <u>1095</u>

- The burning of the Talmud in <u>1242</u>

- In <u>1290</u>, the signature of the edict by King <u>Edward I</u> expelling the Jews from <u>England</u>

- The <u>Alhambra decree</u> was put into effect, leading to the Jewish expulsion from <u>Spain</u> in <u>1492</u>

- The <u>First World War</u> started in <u>1914</u>

- The first killings at <u>Treblinka</u> took place in <u>1942</u>

The purpose of the day is not to institute annual commemorations of historical disasters. Rather, they are commemorated on Tisha B'Av. Examples are the destruction of many Jewish communities in the <u>Rhineland</u> during the <u>Crusades</u>. The liturgy often makes mention of specific instances (see next page).

# HOLOCAUST (SHOAH)

Most <u>Haredi</u> and centrist Orthodox Jews also see Tisha B'Av as a remembrance day for the six million Jews killed by the Nazis during the <u>Holocaust</u>. <u>Modern Orthodox</u> and non-Orthodox Jews remember these on a special day instituted by the government of Israel, called <u>Yom HaShoah</u>. Haredi rabbinical leaders view the institution of a new permanent day of mourning or celebration in our times as anti-traditional, which is why Haredi Jews do not observe <u>Yom Hazikaron</u> either. There are also many who see Tisha B'Av as a remembrance day for the Holocaust as well as participate in its remembrance on Yom HaShoah."[58]

Some of these later day calamities that happened on this date may need a little explanation for the Gentile reader. The Crusades that started on the 9th of Av in 1095 were wars launched to bring the Holy Land under control of the Catholic Church. This Crusade and later Crusades caused widespread slaughter of the Jewish people. Horrible atrocities were committed in the name of Christ. It's been told that the Crusaders played games of seeing how many Jewish babies could be impaled on one's sword. [59]

On the 9th of Av in 1290, the signing of the edict by King Edward I of England brought about the expulsion of some 16,000 Jews and resulted in the loss of most of their property and holdings. They were told to convert to Christianity or leave with the loss of all they owned.

On the 9th of Av in 1492, the Alhambra decree did almost the same thing to all Jews living in Spain. They were told to convert to Christianity or leave with loss of all possessions. Those not converting or not leaving after the deadline were put to death.

On the 9th of Av in 1914, the First World War started. The issues of the First World War were never settled after the war and that lead to World War II and the Holocaust. Six million Jewish men, women and children were exterminated in Hitler's death camps as part of his "Final Solution".

On the 9th of Av, in 1942, the first of many executions started at Treblinka. Executions continued there and at other death camps until the end of the war.

We could go on and on by bringing the sorrowful events up to date but that's enough of the bad things. Let's get back to our study of the Feasts and the good things that are coming.

# CHAPTER FIVE ENDNOTES

54. Esther 3:12-13

55. Esther 4:16

56. Esther 7:9-10

57. Edward Chumney. The Seven Festivals of the Messiah. © 1994, p.62- Destiny Image, Shippenburg, Pa.

58. Wikipedia contributors, Tisha B'Av, Wikipedia, The Free Encyclopedia, <http://en.wikipedia.org/wiki/Tisha_B'Av>[accessed 6 November 2006]

59. Chuck Missler. Isaiah commentary.

# CHAPTER SIX

## THE FALL FEASTS

In our study of the 7 Feasts, we have seen how past events in God's work with man seem to follow the dates of the Spring Feasts. As we examine the Fall Feasts, however, there is a strong indication that this pattern does not continue. For this reason, we consider the Fall Feasts unfulfilled in a general sense but there does seem to be indications that God has begun working His Plan with the Fall Feasts as He has done with the Spring Feasts. For this reason, I believe we can regard the Fall Feasts as prophecy of things to come and destinations ahead of us on the roadmap of God's work with mankind.

Any study of prophecy is always influenced by the writer's basic beliefs and this study is no different. This might be a good place to explain my beliefs on end time prophecy. As you have already concluded from earlier chapters in this book, I believe in a pre-tribulation rapture of the church. Let me further explain my beliefs in relation to God's work with the nation of Israel and His Chosen People. These beliefs are mine and are not without controversy. Many respected theologians and scholars do not agree with my beliefs concerning these end-time events.

There is a concept being taught in our seminaries in most denominations today called, "Replacement Theology". It is, simply stated, the concept that because the Jews rejected Jesus as their Messiah, God's Chosen People, the Jews, have been replaced by the Church in God's Plan and He has turned His Back on the Jews. In other words, the Church has taken over the Jews role in God's Plan. I believe this concept is in error. Before 1948, when the nation of Israel was reborn after 2500+ years, the concept of Replacement Theology had a stronger argument. Since then, we have begun to see how historical events are revealing God's work with the Jews **and** the Church.

I base my belief partially on Paul's statement in Romans 11:

> *For I would not, brethren, that ye should be igno-rant of this mystery, lest ye should be wise in your own conceits; that blindness in part is happened to Israel, **until the fullness of the Gentiles be come in.** And so all Israel shall be saved: as it is witten, There shall come out of Sion the Deliverer, and shall turn away ungodliness from Jacob: For this [is] my covenant unto them, when I shall take away their sins. As concerning the gospel, [they are] enemies for your sakes: but as touching the election, [they are] beloved for the fathers' sakes.*
> (Romans 11:25-28 AV, emphasis mine)

What does, *"until the fullness of the Gentiles be come in."* mean? I believe it refers to the "Church Age" or the "Age of Grace" in which we now live. This age or dispen-sation is the time God is working to bring in the Gentile Church. The Jews are now, as a whole, blinded to the fact that Jesus Christ was and is the Messiah prophesied by their Old Testament.

In Hebrews 8 we find a reference to a "New Covenant":

*"For finding fault with them, he saith, Behold, the days come, saith the Lord, when I will make a **new covenant** with the house of Israel and with the house of Judah: **Not according to the covenant** that I made with their fathers in the day when I took them by the hand to lead them out of the land of Egypt; because they continued not in my covenant, and I regarded them not, saith the Lord. For this [is] the covenant that I will make with the house of Israel after those days, saith the Lord; I will put my laws into their mind, and write them in their hearts: and I will be to them a God, and they shall be to me a people.*

(Hebrews 8:8-10 AV, emphasis mine)

The Orthodox Jews today are not operating under a "New Covenant' but are operating under the covenant described as the one given *"when I took them by the hand to lead them out of the land of Egypt "*. This time of the "New Covenant" is a future time period or dispensation. I believe this present age of when the "fullness of the gentiles be come in" will end with the "catching away" or "rapture" of the Church as written in I Corinthians 15:51-52 and 1 Thessalonians 4:13-17. At that time, God will remove the blindness from the Jews, and they will, as a whole, accept Jesus Christ as their Messiah, and God will use the Jews to evangelize the world left behind at the rapture of the Church.

Does that mean there is another way for a Jew to be saved? No. It does not. Here is what Paul had to say about that in the book of Galatians:

> *There is neither Jew nor Greek, there is neither bond nor free, there is neither male nor female: for ye are all one in Christ Jesus.*
> (Galatians 3:28 AV)

Jesus said in John 14:

> *Jesus saith unto him, I am the way, the truth, and the life: no man cometh unto the Father, but by me.*
> (John 14:6 AV)

The greater part of the Orthodox Jews are today supernaturally blinded to the fact that Jesus Christ was and is the Messiah of the Jews and the Gentiles as well. Orthodox Jews, who accept Jesus Christ as their Messiah now, come into the Church the same as a Gentile believer; by accepting Jesus Christ individually as their Savior and Lord. After the rapture has occurred and God removes the blindness from the Jews, they will each individually accept Jesus Christ as Savior just as is required now. When this happens, the Bible prophecies that virtually all of the Orthodox Jews will profess Jesus Christ as Savior and Lord. God will then use them to preach the gospel to the people left on the earth. I believe this period of time will be 7 years and will also be a time of great tribulation. After this period of time, Jesus will return physically and establish His Kingdom on earth with Jerusalem as His Throne.

There are many different beliefs in the body of Christ on exactly how end time events will play out. I have mine and others I highly respect have differing beliefs. We all have our interpretation of the scriptures and we should be able to disagree in our belief of the details of these events without being disagreeable and causing strife in the body of Christ.

However, this concept of "Replacement Theology" is more serious than just a disagreement in the order of things. God told Abraham and later Abraham's descendents, Isaac and Jacob, what He would do through and with their descendents. These promises are recorded all through the Old Testament. Throughout the New Testament, there are many instances of God making promises of future things He will do through the Jews. The angel Gabriel promised Mary when he told her about the Child to be born to her that some day The Child would sit on the Throne of David. That is a Jewish Throne. That event has not happened yet but God says through the angel Gabriel that it will happen. I believe God says what He means and means what He says. God is not through with the Jews. His work with them is only in a "time out" period during this present age or dispensation. When the rapture of the Church occurs, the Jews will then be the people God uses to evangelize the people left on the earth. The gospel they then will be preaching is the same gospel we preach now; that salvation is only by belief in Jesus Christ of Nazareth, the Promised Messiah, Yeshua of the Old Testament, the Son of God and the Savior of all who believe in His Death, Burial and Resurrection, repent of their sins, and call upon His Name.[60]

There are several scriptures that I believe might apply to teachers of Replacement Theology who say the Church has become the Jews in God's Plan: The first is God's promise to Abraham and his descendents:

> *And I will bless them that bless thee, and curse him that curseth thee: and in thee shall all families of the earth be blessed.*
>
> (Genesis 12:3 AV)

In Revelation the church at Smyrna is warned:

> *I know thy works, and tribulation, and poverty, (but thou art rich) and [I know] the blasphemy of* ***them which say they are Jews, and are not,*** *but [are] the synagogue of Satan.*
>
> (Revelation 2:9 AV, emphasis mine)

In this case and the case following, Jesus is speaking to churches or people who call themselves believers but are committing what He calls "blasphemy".

Also in Revelation the church at Philadelphia is warned:

> *Behold, I will make them of the synagogue of Satan,* ***which say they are Jews, and are not,*** *but do lie; behold, I will make them to come and worship before thy feet, and to know that I have loved thee.*
>
> (Revelation 3:9 AV, emphasis mine)

What really scares me about this concept or belief is that a great many in the Church today are taught and believe that the Church has replaced the Jews in God's Plan and Christians have no obligation or interest in either Israel or the Jews. The scripture about blessing them that bless Israel and the Jews and cursing them that curse

Israel and the Jews is God's Word and it is still in effect today in the lives of individuals, Churches, or nations. My prayer is that our great nation continues to bless Israel and remain her ally so we can remain a great nation and be blessed as we have been in the past.

OK. Now I'll quit preaching and we'll get back to the prophecy of the Fall Feasts.

If you or I were traveling today on our highway system on a road not familiar to us we would, more than likely, be consulting a map to show us destinations ahead of us. I believe the Fall Feasts are destinations ahead of us on God's Roadmap for mankind. If we were traveling on an unfamiliar highway, toward a destination shown on a roadmap, we would begin seeing signs advertising motels, restaurants and other businesses in the upcoming city. As we got closer to the unfamiliar city, we might even see buildings or water towers in the distance indicating that the destination was near. As we got very close to the city, we would begin to notice speed zones and city limit signs. I regard some of the following signs as indications that the destinations symbolized by the Fall Feasts are very near and we are aware that we are very close to arriving at our next destination on God's Roadmap.

**The Fall Feasts unfulfilled except for possibly:**

1. The Birth of Jesus:

Most scholars agree that Jesus was likely born in the early fall and very likely on one of the Fall Feast days. Since the period of time between all 3 of the Fall Feasts is only about 15 days in the Jewish month of Tishiri, known information from the Scriptures cannot pin down the date of Jesus' birth exactly.

In my opinion, if you use the themes of the Fall Feasts as a guide, it would seem to suggest that both the birth and coming return of Jesus the Messiah for His Church did and will occur on Rosh Hashanah / Feast of Trumpets. Several other respected scholars make an excellent case for Jesus' birth on the Feast of Tabernacles/Booths or even Yom Kippur/Day of Atonement. Do your research and form your opinion. No one knows for sure, even though some of us think we do.

The year of His birth is also not certain. Because of irregularities in our calendar, His Birth could have occurred from 8 BC to 3 AD, depending on what source is researched.

One of the most interesting theories on the time of Jesus' Birth combines both Bible information and the latest computer programming that is used in our space program. For astronomers to know the precise position of any planet or star at a future time, a computer program had to be written that would track the movements of all known heavenly bodies both in the future and in the past. The New Testament records the story of the wise men who "followed the star" just after the Birth of Jesus and Revelation 12 records positions of the stars and moon when the child is born to the woman. By using the computer space program to trace back the positions of the moon and stars, star movements and astronomical events of that period in time were re-created by computer and used to control the star illustrations in a planetarium.

In his book, *"The Star That Astonished The World* "Dr. Earnest Martin, using the New Testament accounts of Jesus' Birth, the signs of Revelation 12 and modern astronomy, has shown what appears to be confirmation that Jesus was born on **September 11, of 3 BC**, between the hours of 6:15 and 7:45 PM. Rosh Hashanah/Feast of Trumpets began at twilight of that day.[61]

This book was released some 5 years before **September 11, 2001** changed our lives in these United States completely. If Dr. Martin is correct on the birthdate of Jesus, the events of **September 11, 2001** happened on the anniversary of the birthdate of Jesus by our calendar. I would I would not even make a guess as to the significance of that and will leave any conclusions as to why the events happened on that date to you, the reader.

2. Moses' descent from the mountain with the second set of stone tablets.

Exodus relates the story of how Moses came down the mountain with the first stone tablets and found the children of Israel worshipping a golden calf. In his disgust and anger, he dashed the first set of stone tablets on the ground and broke them. Later he ascended the mountain again and God gave him a second set of stone tablets.

Moses went up Mt. Sinai the 2nd time on the first day of Elul, remained there in the presence of God for 40 days, and descended to a forgiven people on Yom Kippur/Day of Atonement.[62]

3. According to Jewish tradition, Adam sinned and was forgiven, all on the first day of his creation which was Rosh Hashanah/Feast of Trumpets. [63]

4. Also, according to Jewish tradition, the sacrifice of Isaac took place on Rosh Hashanah/Feast of Trumpets providing even more reason for the Rabbis to believe this was the Day of Judgment.

*"The offspring of Isaac will someday transgress my will, and I will judge them on Rosh Hashanah. Should they appeal to my leniency, I will recall the binding of Isaac and let them blow then the horn of this ram [which was substituted for Isaac]" (Tanchuma, Vayero 22:13).*

As we can see from these passages, the rabbis express confidence in God's mercy. For even though a man is judged on Rosh Hashanah, he should be confident that just as God forgave Adam and spared the life of Isaac, he too will gain a favorable decree before his Maker (Tanchuma, Vayero 22:13).[64]

5. Jewish tradition says that either the Prophet Samuel was born on Rosh Hashana/Feast of Trumpets or that was the day that God heard his mother's (Hannah's) prayers for a son. [65]

# CHAPTER SIX ENDNOTES

60. See 1Cor. 15:1-8 for a scriptural definition of the Gospel.

61. Ernest L. Martin," The Star That Astonished The World", Ask Publications, © Ernest L. Martin, 1996.

62. Exodus 34:29

63. Mitch and Zhava Glasner, The Fall Feasts of Israel, Page 45-46, © 1987 Reprinted by permission from Moody Publishers of Chicago

64. Mitch and Zhava Glasner, The Fall Feasts of Israel, Page 45-46, © 1987 Reprinted by permission from Moody Publishers of Chicago

65. 1 Samuel 1:2-10

# CHAPTER SEVEN

## THE FIRST OF THE FALL FEASTS:
### ROSH HASHANAH/FEAST OF TRUMPETS
### UNFULFILLED AND PROPHETIC

*And the LORD spake unto Moses, saying, 'Speak
unto the children of Israel, saying, In the seventh
month, in the first day of the month, shall ye have
a Sabbath, a memorial of blowing of trumpets,
an holy convocation. Ye shall do no servile work
therein: but ye shall offer an offering made by fire
unto the LORD.'*

(Leviticus 23:23-25)

*And in the seventh month, on the first day of the
month, ye shall have an holy convocation; ye
shall do no servile work: it is a day of blowing the
trumpets unto you. (Sacrifices etc.)*

(Numbers 29:1-2)

- 7th month is Tishri, recognized by the appearance of the new moon. (After Exodus 12, when
  the Jews came out of Egypt, only the Jews
  Religious Calendar is used in the Bible text.)

- The second day of the celebration was added
  later, perhaps in Babylon, because of the time

*133*

required for the priests to certify the new moon.

- In Jesus' time and today, it is celebrated for 2 days: Tishri 1 and Tishri 2. The Rabbis count it as one long day.

- It begins the period of time known as "The High Holy Days", or "The Days of Awe" to the Jews. The suggestion in the Hebrew is "Days of Sifting or Threshing". This period ends with Yom Kippur on the 10th of Tishri.

- The period of time begins on Tishri 1 and ends on Tishri 10 but the interval between is 7 days.

**ROSH HASHANAH          YOM KIPPUR**

<u>1</u>          <u>2</u> 3 4 5 6 7 8 9 <u>10</u>

By counting the first and second day as one long day, the interval between Rosh Hashanah and Yom Kippur is 7 days. One of the themes of Rosh Hashanah is the Coronation of the Messiah. One of the themes of Yom Kippur is the physical coming of the Messiah to set up His earthly kingdom. This seven day interval between the two feasts seems to symbolize the 7 years of the "Great Tribulation". I believe the Great Tribulation will begin with the rapture of the church on Rosh Hashanah and will end with the coming of Jesus to establish His earthly kingdom in Jerusalem on Yom Kippur. During this 7 year period of time, I believe the people left on the earth will go through the great Tribulation while the church will be attending the Wedding Supper of the Lamb.

# ROSH HASHANAH/FEAST OF TRUMPETS

- **Actions:**

**(A) Blow the Trumpet. Leviticus 23:24 Numbers 29:1**

  - **Hebrew word for trumpet is Shofar and is a goat's horn not a silver trumpet.**

  - **The three times a year the Shofar is blown are:**

**1. On the Feast of Weeks (Pentecost)**

  - **It's the left horn of the ram and the Jews call it "The First Trump".**

*And **when the voice of the trumpet sounded long**, and waxed louder and louder, Moses spake, and God answered him by a voice.*
(Exodus 19:19, emphasis mine)

  - **It was blown when God gave the Law.**

**2. On the Feast of Trumpets (Rosh Hashanah)**

  - **It's the right horn of the ram and the Jews call it "The Last Trump".**

*Behold, I shew you a mystery; We shall not all sleep, but we shall all be changed, In a moment, in the twinkling of an eye, **at the last trump**: for the trumpet shall sound, and the dead shall be raised incorruptible, and we shall be changed.*
(1 Corinthians 15:51-52, emphasis mine)

*135*

*For the Lord himself shall descend from heaven with a shout, with the voice of the archangel, **<u>and with the trump of God</u>**: and the dead in Christ shall rise first: Then we which are alive and remain shall be caught up together with them in the clouds, to meet the Lord in the air: and so shall we ever be with the Lord.*

(1 Thessalonians 4:16, emphasis mine)

- **The theme of Rosh Hashanah suggests the Rapture will occur on this Feast Day.**

### 3. On the Feast of Atonement (Yom Kippur)

- **The Jews call it "The Great Trump".**

*"And then shall appear the sign of the Son of man in heaven: and then shall all the tribes of the earth mourn, and they shall see the Son of man coming in the clouds of heaven with power and great glory. And he shall send his angels **<u>with a great sound of a trumpet</u>**, and they shall gather together his elect from the four winds, from one end of heaven to the other.*

(Matthew 24:30, emphasis mine)

- **The theme of Yom Kippur suggests that Jesus will physically return on this Feast Day to set up His kingdom.**

- **Actions:**

**(B) Priests offer sacrifices.**

*And ye shall offer a burnt offering for a sweet savour unto the LORD; <u>**one young bullock, one ram, and seven lambs of the first year without blemish:**</u> And their <u>**meat offering shall be of flour mingled with oil, three tenth deals for a bullock, and two tenth deals for a ram,**</u> And <u>**one tenth deal for one lamb, throughout the seven lambs:**</u> And <u>**one kid of the goats for a sin offering**</u>, to make an atonement for you: Beside the burnt offering of the month, and his meat offering, and the daily burnt offering, and his meat offering, and their drink offerings, according unto their manner, for a sweet savour, a sacrifice made by fire unto the LORD.*

(Numbers 29:2-6, emphasis mine)

● **Actions:**

**(C) A time of self-evaluation.**

- ● **Elul, the entire preceding month, is a time of repentance.**

- ● **Many go to public baths or "mikvah" for ritual cleansing.**

● **Actions:**

**(D) Observe as a Sabbath day.**

- ● **May occur on any day of the week. Determined by date. It occurs on Tishiri 1 of the Jews calendar.**

*Ye shall do no servile work therein.*

(Leviticus 23:25)

# ROSH HASHANAH/FEAST OF TRUMPETS

### Names, Themes and Idioms

The Jews have many names for this feast day and each of the names has a suggestion of a theme or idiom concerning this feast.

One of the names for this feast day is **Teshuvah (Repentance)** and it is considered by the Jews as a day of repentance. The entire month preceding this feast day, the month of Elul, is set aside for repentance and cleansing. Many would go to public baths or "mikvah" for ritual cleansing. This process is probably the Old Testament version of the water baptism practiced by New Testament Christians.

Another name for this feast is **Rosh Hashanah (Head of the Year, Birthday of the World).** Jews believe it to be the very day when God created Adam. Tishri was the first month of the year on the old or Secular Calendar. They believe that their calendar, with New Year on this day, reflects the actual number of years since Adam's creation. In 2006 and 2007 on our calendar, it will be 5767 on the Jew's calendar. The Jews believe that this is the actual number of years since Adam's creation. Many Gentile scholars, however, think this number is too low and needs to be increased by a few hundred years to reflect the actual time elapsed since the creation. Their reasoning for this

**138**

disagreement with the Jewish Rabbis is that in the Old Testament, several of the genealogies seem to skip from grandfather to grandson rather than from father to son and these genealogies are used by the Rabbis to compute the years since Adam. There is no agreement among Old Testament scholars as to the correct number of years to add to the Jews calendar but the true years since Adam's creation would appear to be close to 6000.

Another name for this feast is **Yom Teruah (the Day of the Awakening Blast\Feast of Trumpets)**. The Old Testament and Jewish writings teach of a day when the graves will open and a great resurrection will occur.

> *Martha saith unto him, I know that he shall rise again in the resurrection at the last day. Jesus said unto her, 'I am the resurrection, and the life: he that believeth in me, though he were dead, yet shall he live.'*
>
> (John 11:24-25 AV)

Martha is quoting an Old Testament teaching since the New Testament as we know it, was not written at that time.

The suggestion in name of the Awakening Blast/Feast of Trumpets is that the resurrection will occur on this day. The theme of rapture (natzal) is also associated with this feast day. Since the New Testament teaches of the catching away or rapture of the church and the resurrection occurring at the "Last Trump", this seems a strong suggestion of both of those events occurring on this feast day. I believe that is the next destination on God's Roadmap for mankind.

This feast is also called **Yom HaDin (The Day of Judgment)** by the Jews with the suggestion that God will judge all mankind on this day. If Jesus the Messiah returns for His Church on this day, then that future day will become the day that God will judge all living men by their relationship with Jesus Christ.

Yet another name for the feast is **HaMelech (the Coronation of the Messiah)** with the suggestion that Yeshua (the Promised Messiah of the Old Testament) will be crowned on this day. If Jesus' Birth occurred on this feast day as I believe it did, He was physically ordained by God as Messiah on this day just as the angel told Mary.

Another name is **Yom HaZakkaron (the Day of Remembrance or Memorial)**.

It is also called **The Time of Jacob's Trouble (the birth pangs of the Messiah).** The Time of Jacob's Trouble is associated with the time period we call The Great Tribulation[66] and suggests Messiah coming forth at this time.

It is also called **Kiddushin/Nesu'in (the wedding ceremony)** in Jewish culture. In a Jewish wedding procedure, the groom pays a dowry and makes a contract with the bride's father for the bride. He then goes to build a house and prepare a place for them to live. When the new house is ready, he returns for the bride and takes her away with him. What a fitting day for Jesus the Messiah and Bridegroom to return for His Bride, the Church.

It is called **The Last Trump (Shofar).** I believe Paul is giving us a clue as to when the "rapture" or "catching away" of the Church will occur.  To a Jew, this was like saying it would occur sometime in the future on this feast day.

> *Behold, I shew you a mystery; We shall not all sleep, but we shall all be changed, In a moment, in the twinkling of an eye, **at the last trump:** for the trumpet shall sound, and the dead shall be raised incorruptible, and we shall be changed.*
> (1Corinthians 15:51-52 AV, emphasis mine)

> *For the Lord himself shall descend from heaven with a shout, with the voice of the archangel, and **with the trump of God**: and the dead in Christ shall rise first.*
> (1 Thessalonians 4:16 AV, emphasis mine)

It is called **Yom Hakeseh (the Hidden Day)**.  This feast day occurs on Tishri 1 and the beginning of Tishri is determined by the position of the moon.  The Priests have to certify that the moon is in a certain position before the Shofar can be blown and the day certified as the feast day.  I'm told that in Jewish culture that almost everyone knows when the moon is in the right position to call it Tishri 1 and it is certainly no surprise when the priests certify the day and the Shofar blows.

If one Jew asked another how long it was to this feast day, a common reply would be," The day is hidden.  No man knows the day or the hour."  This would be followed by a wink.

Yes, it is a hidden day but there are many clues and suggestions as to when it will occur.  The message to you and I would seem to be: "Wake up.  Look around you.  See how world events are shaping up. The day is hidden, but those who are aware know the time is near." We don't know exactly how close we are to this destination, but I believe it is the next stop on God's Roadmap for mankind.

# 16 REASONS FOR THE BLOWING OF THE SHOFAR

1. The Torah was given to Israel with the sound of the shofar (Exodus [Shemot] 19:19).

2. Israel conquered in the battle of Jericho with the blast of the shofar (Joshua 6:20).

3. Israel will be advised of the advent of the Messiah with the sound of the shofar (Zechariah 9:14, 16).

4. The shofar will be blown at the time of the ingathering of the exiles of Israel to their place (Isaiah [Yeshayahu] 27:13).

5. The shofar was blown to signal the assembly of the Israelites during war (Judges [Shoftim] 3:27; 2 Samuel 20:1).

6. The watchman who stood upon Jerusalem's walls blew the shofar (Ezekiel [Yechezekel] 33:3-6).

7. The shofar was blown at the start of the Jubilee year (Leviticus [Vayikra] 25:9).

8. The shofar is a reminder that G-d is sovereign (Psalm [Tehillim] 47:5).

9. The ram's horn, the shofar, is a reminder of Abra-

ham's sacrifice of Isaac and G-d's provision of a ram as a substitute (Genesis [Bereishit] 22:13).

10. The shofar was blown to announce the beginning of festivals (Numbers [Bamidbar] 10:10). The shofar was blown to celebrate the new moon on Rosh HaShanah (Psalm 81:1-3).

11. The blowing of the shofar is a signal for the call to repentance (Isaiah [Yeshayahu] 58:1).

12. The blowing of the shofar ushers in the day of the L-rd (Joel 2:1).

13. The blowing of the shofar is sounded at the rapture of the believers and the resurrection of the dead (1 Thessalonians 4:16).

14. John was taken up to Heaven in the Book of Revelation by the sound of the shofar (Revelation 4:1).

15. Seven shofarim are sounded when G-d judges the earth during the tribulation (Revelation 8-9).

16. The shofar was used for the coronation of kings (1 Kings [Melachim] 1:34, 39).[67]

# CHAPTER SEVEN ENDNOTES

66. Jeremiah 30:7

67. Materials from "The Seven Festivals of the Messiah", by Edward Chumney, copyright 1994, used by permission of Destiny Image Publishers, 167 Walnut Bottom Road, Shippensburg, PA 17257 www.destinyimage.com

# CHAPTER EIGHT

## YOM KIPPUR OR DAY OF ATONEMENT

### UNFULFILLED AND PROPHETIC

*And this shall be a statute for ever unto you: that in the **seventh month, on the tenth day of the month,** ye shall afflict your souls, and do no work at all, whether it be one of your own country, or a stranger that sojourneth among you:*

*For **on that day shall the priest make an atonement for you,** to cleanse you, that ye may be clean from all your sins before the LORD. It shall be a Sabbath of rest unto you, and ye shall afflict your souls, by a statute for ever. And the priest, whom he shall anoint, and whom he shall consecrate to minister in the priest's office in his father's stead, shall make the atonement, and shall put on the linen clothes, even the holy garments: And he shall make an atonement for the holy sanctuary, and he shall make an atonement for the tabernacle of the congregation, and for the altar, and he shall make an atonement for the priests, and for all the people of the congregation. And this shall be an everlasting statute unto you, to make an atonement*

*for the children of Israel for all their sins **once a
year**. And he did as the LORD commanded Moses.*
(Leviticus 16:29-34, emphasis mine)

*Also on the tenth day of this seventh month there
shall be a day of atonement: it shall be an holy convocation unto you; and ye shall afflict your souls,
and offer an offering made by fire unto the LORD.
And ye shall do no work in that same day: for it is
a day of atonement, to make an atonement for you
before the LORD your God. For whatsoever soul it
be that shall not be afflicted in that same day, he
shall be cut off from among his people. And whatsoever soul it be that doeth any work in that same
day, the same soul will I destroy from among his
people. Ye shall do no manner of work: it shall be
a statute for ever throughout your generations in
all your dwellings. It shall be unto you a Sabbath
of rest, and ye shall afflict your souls: in the ninth
day of the month at even, from even unto even, shall
ye celebrate your Sabbath.*
(Leviticus 23:27-32)

- **Yom Kippur/Day of Atonement is a one day
  period observed on the 10th day of Tishri.**

- **This was the only day of the year that the
  High Priest and no other priest but the High
  Priest, after elaborate sacrifice and cleansing,
  entered into the Holy of Holies and came face
  to face with the Presence of God.**

The Holy of Holies was separated by a veil and could be
entered only by the High Priest, only on Yom Kippur/Day
of Atonement, and only after an elaborate washing and
cleansing procedure. Since no other priest could enter, the

High Priest wore bells on his garment and had a rope attached to his leg so the other priests could drag him out of the Holy of Holies if something had not been done correctly and God struck him dead or if he died a natural death while behind the veil. I can find no instance of this occurring in recorded Jewish history. It was evidently part of the priests "what if" plan in carrying out the details of the feast day. The Presence of God was behind the veil and no one other than the High Priest on this one day was allowed to go into the Presence of God no matter what the circumstances.

● **This was the only day of the year that the High Priest was allowed to speak aloud the name of God. (YHVH) A name so holy and revered that since Moses, no man has known exactly how to pronounce it.**

In the Hebrew language, there are no written vowels and pronunciation is by interpretation. The name of God was so holy that no Jew could ever speak the name of God and the High Priest could only speak it three times in ceremonies on this day once a year. Each time he spoke the name of God aloud during the ceremonies, the people fell to the ground on their faces and replied in Hebrew a phrase that is translated as, **"Blessed be the Name of the radiance of the Kingship, forever and beyond."**[68]

To this day, Orthodox Jews do not speak or write the name of God. In my quotes from Jews in this book, you may have noticed the word "God" written as "G-d" and "Lord" written as "L-rd". Even though the writers I quote are Messianic Jews, they do this also so as not to offend their Orthodox Jewish readers.

**147**

Moses knew how to pronounce the name of God but because it was pronounced so seldom, and then by the High Priest alone, the correct pronunciation was lost. When Jesus returns as High Priest and King on this day in the future, He **will** pronounce it correctly.

- **This was the only day of the year that the procedure of the scapegoat (azazel) was carried out.**[69]

Two goats were chosen as a sin sacrifice. One to sacrifice for the sins of the people and one to turn loose in the wilderness to represent the people's sins being carried far away from them. The High Priest drew lots for the goats and the one whose lot was drawn was sacrificed and the blood sprinkled on the Mercy Seat in the Holy of Holies as atonement for the sins of the people. The High Priest then took some of the blood of the goat sacrificed as a sin offering for the people, and some of the blood of the bull he sacrificed earlier as a sin offering for the High Priest and his household, and smeared the blood of the bull and the goat on the horns of the second, living goat. He also then attached a piece of scarlet thread to the horn of the second goat and tied a piece of the same thread to the handle of the door to the Temple. The second goat was then set free in the wilderness symbolizing the people's sins being carried far away from them.

Sometime later, when the second goat had perished in the wilderness, the scarlet thread tied to the handle of the door to the Temple turned white as a sign that the sacrifice had been accepted by God.

- **This was the only day of the year when all sacrifices and ceremonies had to be performed by the High Priest in person.**

All priests had to be of the tribe of Levi, but the High Priest must not only be of the tribe of Levi, but he must also be a descendent of Aaron. This was the only feast of the year when all the sacrifices and actions in the Temple had to be performed by the High Priest in person. [70]

In Jesus' time, the Romans had appointed Caiaphas as High Priest. Caiaphas was not of the line of Aaron so he was a counterfeit High Priest. The trial and crucifixion of Jesus was illegal in many ways under Jewish law and was conducted by an illegal High Priest.

- **This was a national day of fasting. Leviticus 23:27, "ye shall afflict your souls."**

Yom Kippur/Day of Atonement is the only day of the year proclaimed by scripture to be a fast day. It is a day for fasting and presenting your sins to God and asking that the blood of the sacrifices cover your sins for another year.

This explanation of the actions of Yom Kippur/Day of Atonement might be a good place to explain the difference between the words, "atonement" and "remission" from a scriptural point of view.

The word "atonement" is used almost exclusively in the Old Testament as God's way of dealing with the sins of the people. It means "to cover over and remove from sight". When the blood of the bulls and goats was poured out on the Mercy Seat in Old Testament times on the Day of

Atonement, it did not remove the sins of the people; it only covered over the sins for another year. It was much like painting a house with another color. The old color is covered over nicely when it is first applied, but before long, the original color begins to show through. It has to be re-applied. The blood of bulls and goats did not remove sin, it only covered-up sin for a season and then it must be re-applied.

The word "remission" is a New Testament word and means, "to remove as if it never existed". It is used in the New Testament to describe how Jesus' Blood handles sin. It doesn't just cover sin. It completely removes it as if it never existed.

Jesus is described by John the Baptist as the Lamb of God who came to take away the sins of the world. His Blood was not shed for the <u>atonement</u> of sin. It was shed for the <u>remission</u> of sin.

> *For the law having a shadow of good things to come, [and] not the very image of the things, can never with those sacrifices which they offered year by year continually make the comers thereunto perfect. For then would they not have ceased to be offered? Because that the worshippers once purged should have had no more conscience of sins. But in those [sacrifices there is] a remembrance again [made] of sins every year. For [it is] not possible that the blood of bulls and of goats should take away sins.*
>
> (Hebrews 10:1-4 AV)

> *But into the second [went] the high priest alone once every year, not without blood, which he*

**150**

*offered for himself, and [for] the errors of the people.*

(Hebrews 9:7 AV)

*But Christ being come an high priest of good things to come, by a greater and more perfect tabernacle, not made with hands, that is to say, not of this building; Neither by the blood of goats and calves, but by his own blood he entered in once into the holy place, having obtained eternal redemption [for us].*

(Hebrews 9:11-12 AV)

For the believer, Jesus' Blood removes the believer's sins as if they had never been committed.

*But this man, after he had offered one sacrifice for sins for ever, sat down on the right hand of God.*

(Hebrews 10:12 AV)

*For this is my blood of the new testament, which is shed for many for the remission of sins.*

(Matthew 26:28 AV)

*And almost all things are by the law purged with blood; and without shedding of blood is no remission.*

(Hebrews 9:22 AV)

- **Yom Kippur/Day of Atonement was the beginning day of a Jubilee year. Leviticus 25:8-9.**

In Leviticus 25, God set up the year of the Jubilee. It was to occur every 50 years. It was a time in when all debts were cancelled, bondservants were freed, and no crops were planted. God provided that in the preceding year, crops would increase to the point of having more than enough food for the Jubilee year without working. If land had been sold or mortgaged, it must be returned to the original owner. This Jubilee year began and ended not by the New Year on either the Secular or Religious calendar, but on Yom Kippur/Day of Atonement.

In Luke 4:18 and 19, and 21, Jesus said,

> *The Spirit of the Lord is upon me, because he hath anointed me to preach the gospel to the poor; he hath sent me to heal the brokenhearted, to preach deliverance to the captives, and recovering of sight to the blind, to set at liberty them that are bruised,* **To preach the acceptable year of the Lord,** *(emphasis mine)*
>
> *And he began to say unto them, This day is this scripture fulfilled in your ears.*

This "acceptable year of the Lord" He spoke of was understood by the Jews to mean a Jubilee year.

There is much symbolism and suggestion in this scripture and elsewhere in the New Testament about Jubilee years. Jesus suggested in the scripture above that this time was upon His listeners.

It is also associated with the 1,000 year period when Jesus will physically return to Planet Earth and rule and reign. The dragon or serpent or satan* will be bound during this time.[71] That is one of the main reasons for the belief that Jesus will physically return on Yom Kippur/Day of Atonement.

For this all to make sense, you have to be aware of a

belief of the Jewish Rabbis and others including myself that I call the "Six Day Theory". Here is a general explanation of it:

In Genesis, it's stated that God created the earth in 6 days and on the 7th day, He rested. This is believed to be an outline of the future. In Psalms we find the scripture saying:

> *For a thousand years in thy sight [are but] as yesterday when it is past, and [as] a watch in the night.*
>
> (Psalm 90:4 AV)

Although the New Testament is not considered scripture by the Orthodox Jewish Rabbis, there is a parallel scripture found in 2 Peter:

> *But, beloved, be not ignorant of this one thing, that one day [is] with the Lord as a thousand years, and a thousand years as one day.*
>
> (2 Peter 3:8 AV)

The belief is that man's dominion on the earth as granted in Genesis would last for 6 "days" or 6,000 years. The coming 1,000 year period is the 7th day when Jesus the Messiah will reign. It is also believed that the scripture in Genesis that states, *"And the LORD said, My spirit shall not always strive with man, for that he also [is] flesh: yet his days shall be an hundred and twenty years." (Genesis 6:3 AV)* suggests 120 Jubilees was man's dominion on Planet Earth. One hundred and twenty Jubilees would be 120 X 50 = 6,000 years. As stated earlier in our discussion on the Jews calendar, we do not know the exact number of years since Adam, but it appears to be very close to 6,000. If that

**153**

is correct, when the 6,000[th] year by God's reckoning does occur, then the dominion of man on this planet will end and the reign of Jesus the Messiah will begin on that particular Yom Kippur/Day of Atonement. I believe that is destination #2 ahead of us on God's Roadmap for mankind.

**Actions all performed by the High Priest with great ceremony on Yom Kippur/Day of Atonement:**

**1. He used a golden censer with incense.**

**New Testament application:** The incense represents the prayers of Bible believers. Psalms 141:2, Luke 1:5-11, Revelation 5:8, 8:3-4.

**2. He went within the veil once a year.**

**New Testament application**: By the Death and Resurrection of our Lord Jesus we are free to enter the veil every day.

When Jesus died on the cross, the New Testament records that the veil of the Temple was torn in two.[72] The Spirit of God dwelled in the Holy of Holies and the veil separated this place from the rest of the Temple. The veil being torn symbolized the opening of the Holy of Holies so that any believer, not just the High Priest, could enter into the Presence of God. The veil was not just some flimsy fabric separating the Holy of Holies. It was a woven fabric that was about as thick as the width of a man's hand (about 4 inches). It was tested by hooking up two yokes of oxen to each end and pulling. If it tore, it was rejected.[73] This is what was split that day when Jesus died.

## 3. He washed himself in water.

After the High Priest had ritually cleansed himself including washing all over, he went immediately into the Holy of Holies to offer the sacrifices. No one touched or handled him after he had performed the cleansing. The picture here is like the doctor going into the operating room after scrubbing up. He would hold up his hands and allow nothing to contaminate him.

Under the New Testament, Jesus is our High Priest.[74] He told Mary when she went to the tomb and found that He had arisen, "Touch me not; for I am not yet ascended to my Father."[75] It appears that Jesus is acting here in His role as High Priest and is about to present His own Blood as a sin sacrifice as well as presenting Himself as the First-fruits.

For you to better understand the Jewish mindset concerning being unclean, let me relate an incident that happened to my wife and me recently.

We were attending a weekend conference for Christians and Jews. In attendance were both Messianic and Orthodox Jews from all around the world. We were seated at tables with 8 to 10 people at each table. Our table was occupied by both Orthodox and Messianic Jews and their spouses as well as some Christian couples. Before the meeting started, we visited with the other couples and introduced ourselves around the table. One of the Orthodox Jewish men politely made this statement to the ladies around our table: "I apologize in advance for not shaking hands with you ladies. I don't intend to be rude but the

Torah teaches that a man is unclean after touching a woman who is menstruating. Since I have no way of knowing which of you ladies might be unclean, I just do not shake hands with any woman." And he didn't! It made us realize just how much freedom we have as New Testament Christians.

> *Christ hath redeemed us from the curse of the law, being made a curse for us: for it is written, Cursed [is] every one that hangeth on a tree.*
> (Galatians 3:13 AV)

I can find no record in the New Testament of Jesus letting <u>anyone</u> touch Him after His Resurrection until the time that He appeared to the disciples and then He encouraged Thomas to feel His wounds. According to John, this was after 8 days.[76] There are differences of opinion as to the significance of the 8 days. According to Numbers 19:11, a Jew was unclean for 7 days after touching a dead body. Eight days was also the time required after birth for the Jewish baby to be circumcised. I'll leave the study of the reason for the 8 days to you, the reader. Whatever the reason, Jesus fulfilled His role as High Priest by allowing <u>no one</u> to touch Him until He ascended to the Father and therefore He was ceremonially clean under the Jewish law as well as being without sin.

**New Testament application:** For Aaron, or any other High Priest, this meant that he had to be absolutely clean in order to make atonement in behalf of the people. For Jesus, it meant he <u>was</u> clean (without sin). For the believer in Jesus, it means we <u>are</u> cleansed by His Blood that washes white as snow.

## 4. He put on white, holy linen garments.

**New Testament application:** The white linen garments of the Priest symbolize righteousness. After the sacrifices were made, the clothes were stained with blood. The Priest then put on new white linen garments. When the believer accepts Jesus as their Lord and Savior, He exchanges our sin stained garments for His garments cleansed forever by His Blood.

5. **At the moment the atonement was made on the Day of Atonement, those being atoned for were sinless and blameless before God.**

**New Testament application:** The congregation (the Jewish Nation) is being presented to God as without spot or blemish.

*Husbands, love your wives, even as Christ also loved the church, and gave himself for it; That he might sanctify and cleanse it with the washing of water by the word, That he might present it to himself a glorious church, not having spot, or wrinkle, or any such thing; but that it should be holy and without blemish.*

(Ephesians 5:25-27 AV)

The New Testament Church is without spot, wrinkle or blemish not because it is sinless and perfect in its actions but because it has been cleansed by the Blood of Jesus.

6. **The bodies of the animals were taken outside the camp.**

**New Testament application:** The bodies of the sin offerings, both the bullock and the goat, were taken outside the camp. Jesus was crucified outside the camp or gates of Jerusalem.

## 7. Many sacrifices were offered.

**New Testament application:** Our bodies are to be a living sacrifice to God.

*I beseech you therefore, brethren, by the mercies of God, that ye present your bodies a living sacrifice, holy, acceptable unto God, [which is] your reasonable service.*

(Romans 12:1 AV)

*Ye also, as lively stones, are built up a spiritual house, an holy priesthood, to offer up spiritual sacrifices, acceptable to God by Jesus Christ.*

(1 Peter 2:5 AV)

## We are to offer up a sacrifice of praise to God.

*By him therefore let us offer the sacrifice of praise to God continually, that is, the fruit of [our] lips giving thanks to his name. But to do good and to communicate forget not: for with such sacrifices God is well pleased.*

(Hebrews 13:15-16 AV)

# YOM KIPPUR OR DAY OF ATONEMENT

## Names, Themes and Idioms

- **Yom Kippur (the Day of Atonement)**
  - **Day the blood was sprinkled on the Mercy Seat for the Atonement of the sins of the people.**

- **Face to Face**
  - **The day when the high Priest met God face to face.**

- **The Day (or the Great Day)**
  - **The Highest, most Holy Day of the year.**

- **The Fast**
  - **The Day of required fasting.**

- **The Great Shofar**
  - **The Great Trump was blown signaling the closing of the gates.**

- **Neilah (the closing of the gates)**
  - **Jew's believe on this day the Book of Life was closed along with the Gates of Heaven.** [77]

# YOM KIPPUR OR DAY OF ATONEMENT

### 4 Ominous Omens occurring before the Temple was destroyed

We cannot complete the study of Yom Kippur/Day of Atonement without relating the story of the 4 ominous omens that began to occur about 40 years before the Temple was destroyed. This story is from the Jewish Rabbi's own writings from that time period and is recorded in the Talmud and Mishna.

To refresh our memory on the history of that time period, the second Temple, built by Herod, was destroyed on the 9th of Av in 70 AD. This destruction was prophesied by Jesus Himself in Luke:

*For the days shall come upon thee, that thine enemies shall cast a trench about thee, and compass thee round, and keep thee in on every side, And shall lay thee even with the ground, and thy children within thee; and they shall not leave in thee one stone upon another; because thou knewest not the time of thy visitation.*

(Luke 19:43-44 AV)

Because of numerous rebellions in Israel, the Roman general Titus laid siege to Jerusalem. Titus had given orders not to destroy the Temple but in the street to street fighting during the final battle for the city, the Temple was set on fire.

The Temple interior was built of cedar overlaid with thin gold. When the Temple burned, the gold melted and ran into the cracks between the huge stones making up the outer wall. After the fire was out, the soldiers tore down the remaining walls and moved every stone of the Temple to get to the gold between and beneath them. Jesus' prophecy was literally fulfilled to the letter. This event was well recorded and became an important landmark in Jewish history. To this day, the Temple has not been rebuilt and the offering of blood sacrifices ceased with the destruction of the Temple.

Jesus' crucifixion occurred in 32 AD by many scholars reckoning. That date is not without controversy as some reckon it to be any year from 29 AD to 34 AD. The Jewish Rabbis who wrote the Mishna and the Talmud did not recognize Jesus as the Messiah and therefore did not connect Jesus' Death with the strange omens that began happening in the Jew's religious practices. Jesus death was recorded in Jewish history by Josephus and others but the Rabbis could not understand how the death of some Jewish rebel named Jesus would affect their ancient ceremonies in the Temple.

Here are the 4 ominous omens that started happening about 40 years before the destruction of the Temple as recorded in writings by the Rabbis:

1.   In the drawing of lots for the scapegoat (azazel), the lot for the Lord's goat (La Adonai) came up in the priest's left hand. This had never happened before and was considered a very bad sign. This happened every year for about 40 years before the destruction of the Temple.

2. The scarlet thread used to put on the scapegoat's horn and also on the door of the Temple, stopped turning white when the scapegoat perished. In the Babylonian Talmud the Rabbis record that this strangely stopped happening about 40 years before the destruction of the Temple.

3. The Westernmost light on the Temple candelabra would not burn. It is believed the light was used in ancient times to light the others. The light quit burning about 40 years before the destruction of the Temple.

4. The Temple doors would open by themselves. This was first noticed about 40 years before the destruction of the Temple. The priests related this to Zechariah 11:1. *"Open thy doors, O Lebanon, that the fire may devour thy cedars."* (Zechariah 11:1 AV) and considered it as prophecy that the Temple would be destroyed by fire.

Why did these things begin happening at that time? Because God had brought about a New Covenant through Jesus Christ the Son about 40 years before the destruction of the Temple in 70 AD.

Was Jesus of Nazareth, who died on the cross on or about 32 AD, the long awaited Messiah for the Jews as well as for the Gentiles? Was He God the Son and the God of Abraham, Isaac and Jacob come in the flesh? That is the very basis for the Christian faith. One would think this evidence alone would be enough to convince anyone that He was.

# CHAPTER EIGHT ENDNOTES

68. Materials from "The Seven Festivals of the Messiah", by Edward Chumney, copyright 1994, used by permission of Destiny Image Publishers, 167 Walnut Bottom Road, Shippensburg, PA 17257 www.destinyimage.com

69. Leviticus 16:7-10

70. Leviticus 16

71. Revelation 20:2.

72. Matthew 27:51, Mark 15:38, Luke 23.45

73. Richard Booker, The Miracle of the Scarlet Thread, Page 69, Destiny Image Publishers, Shippenburg, PA 17257

74. Hebrews 3:1

75. John 20:17

76. John 20:24-27

77. Materials from "The Seven Festivals of the Messiah", by Edward Chumney, copyright 1994, used by permission of Destiny Image Publishers, 167 Walnut Bottom Road, Shippensburg, PA 17257.

# CHAPTER NINE

## THE LAST OF THE
## 7 FEASTS OF ISRAEL

### THE FEAST OF SUKKOT OR TABERNACLES OR BOOTHS

#### UNFULFILLED AND PROPHETIC

*Speak unto the children of Israel, saying, The fifteenth day of this seventh month [shall be] the feast of tabernacles [for] seven days unto the LORD. On the first day [shall be] an holy convocation: ye shall do no servile work [therein]. Seven days ye shall offer an offering made by fire unto the LORD: on the eighth day shall be an holy convocation unto you; and ye shall offer an offering made by fire unto the LORD: it [is] a solemn assembly; [and] ye shall do no servile work [therein]. These [are] the feasts of the LORD, which ye shall proclaim [to be] holy convocations, to offer an offering made by fire unto the LORD, a burnt offering, and a meat offering, a sacrifice, and drink offerings, every thing upon his day: Beside the Sabbaths of the LORD, and beside your gifts, and beside all your vows, and beside all your freewill offerings, which ye give unto the LORD. Also in the fifteenth day of the seventh month, when ye have gathered in the fruit of the land, ye shall keep a feast unto the LORD seven days: on the first day [shall be] a Sabbath, and on the eighth day [shall be] a Sabbath. And ye shall take you on the first day the boughs of goodly trees, branches of palm trees, and the boughs of thick trees, and willows of the brook; and ye shall rejoice before the LORD your God seven days. And ye shall keep it a feast unto the LORD seven days in the year. [It shall be] a statute for ever in your generations: ye shall celebrate it in the seventh month. Ye shall dwell in booths seven days; all that are Israelites born shall dwell in booths: That your generations may know that I made the children of Israel to dwell in booths, when I brought them out of the land of Egypt: I [am] the LORD your God.*

(Leviticus 23:34-43 AV)

### Pilgrim Feast

*Three times in a year shall all thy males appear before the LORD thy God in the place which he shall choose; in the feast of unleavened bread, and in the feast of weeks, and in the feast of tabernacles: and they shall not appear before the LORD empty: Every man [shall give] as he is able, according to the blessing of the LORD thy God which he hath given thee.*

(Deuteronomy 16:16-17 AV)

## Historical Observance

In the book of Nehemiah it is found that the Feast of Tabernacles or Booths was not always observed by the Jews.

*And they found written in the law which the LORD had commanded by Moses, that the children of Israel should dwell in booths in the feast of the seventh month: And that they should publish and proclaim in all their cities, and in Jerusalem, saying, Go forth unto the mount, and fetch olive branches, and pine branches, and myrtle branches, and palm branches, and branches of thick trees, to make booths, as [it is] written. So the people went forth, and brought [them], and made themselves booths, every one upon the roof of his house, and in their courts, and in the courts of the house of God, and in the street of the water gate, and in the street of the gate of Ephraim. And all the congregation of them that were come again out of the captivity made booths, and sat under the booths: for since the days of Joshua the son of Nun unto that day had not the children of Israel done so. And there was very great gladness.*

(Nehemiah 8:14-17 AV)

## Future Observance

In the book of Zechariah we find that the Feast of Tabernacles/Booths <u>will</u> be observed by <u>all</u> nations during the Millennial Reign of Jesus. Should any nation not observe the Feast, the consequences are stated.

**167**

*And it shall come to pass, [that] every one that is left of all the nations which came against Jerusalem shall even go up from year to year to worship the King, the LORD of hosts, and to keep the feast of tabernacles. And it shall be, [that] whoso will not come up of [all] the families of the earth unto Jerusalem to worship the King, the LORD of hosts, even upon them shall be no rain. And if the family of Egypt go not up, and come not, that [have] no [rain]; there shall be the plague, wherewith the LORD will smite the heathen that come not up to keep the feast of tabernacles.*

(Zechariah 14:16-18 AV)

- **It is a "Pilgrim Feast" and requires the presence of every able-bodied Jewish male in Jerusalem.**

We have seen already that 3 feasts every year require the physical presence of every able-bodied Jewish male who claims to be a practicing Orthodox Jew. As we read the prophecy above as set out in the book of Zechariah, we begin to see a hint of why God is requiring the presence of every able-bodied male in Jerusalem during the Old Testament period of time. According to this scripture, during the Millennium, all nations, whether Jew or gentile will observe the Feast of Tabernacles. If they refuse to come to Jerusalem to worship the King (Jesus), no rain will fall on their land. In addition, the families of Egypt will not only receive no rain but will also be struck by the plague.

I must comment on the things we can learn from this scripture that are not readily apparent. It appears that during the Millennium, when Jesus rules and reigns Planet Earth from Jerusalem, mankind will still have the right to make choices. Mankind will still be dependent on God, through nature, to supply the elemental things, such as rain, we need for everyday life. This is a time period when we will virtually be living in heaven on earth. Even though we know that satan (intentionally not capitalized) is bound during this time period,[78] there is still sickness (plague) on the earth. Think of these things that are revealed through this scripture as you think of the traditional picture of heaven. Traditionally, we picture it as men and women with wings, clad in white bathrobes, floating around on clouds strumming harps. This scripture, however, seems to picture a real place, with real people, both resurrected and natural, on an earth not much different from what we experience today living in fellowship with a real Jesus. When Jesus does physically return to Planet Earth for the Millennium, the scriptures teach that we, the Church, will be with Him and will reign with Him.[79]

- **The Feast of Tabernacles or Booths begins on the 15th day of the 7th month (Tishri) of the Jews Religious calendar and lasts for 8 days.**

- **The 1st day and the 8th day are High Holy Days (Shabbatons) and are treated in practice just like a Saturday Sabbath. (No work and limited travel. Travel was limited to 800-900 yards or 2,000 cubits.)**

Actually, when you read the scriptures carefully in Leviticus, God sets up the Feast of Tabernacles for 7 days and then adds on an 8th day which is a High Holy Day

(Shabbaton). The Rabbi's even go so far as to regard the 8th day as a separate Feast Day and call it, **"Shemini Atzeret"** and even add another day to the feast called **"Simchat Torah"**. **This added day is lumped with the 8th day and counted as one long day.**[80] It is a day of rejoicing in the Torah.

Symbolically, the 7 days symbolize the 7,000 years of man's time on the earth, 6,000 years with mankind in a position of dominion and the 1,000 years of the Millennium with Jesus as King. The 8th day symbolizes a "time after time' or eternity in which mankind will live in fellowship with God forever.

- **The 1st and 8th days of the feast may fall on any day of the week. They are determined by date. (15th and 22nd of Tishri) In addition to observing the first and last days of the feast as Sabbaths, any Saturday that falls within this period is also observed as a Sabbath. (No work and limited travel. Travel was limited to 800-900 yards or 2,000 cubits.)**

- **Boughs of trees are waved in rejoicing before the Lord. It is a feast of rejoicing.**

This feast, more than any of the others, is a feast of rejoicing. God is dwelling among men! Every day of the feast, boughs of trees are waved in rejoicing before the Lord.

*And ye shall take you on the first day the boughs of goodly trees, branches of palm trees, and the boughs of thick trees, and willows of the brook;*

*and ye shall rejoice before the LORD your God
seven days.*

(Leviticus 23:40 AV)

The palm branches and the willows are self explanatory but what are the boughs of "goodly" trees and the boughs of "thick" or "leafy" trees? The Rabbis defined three of the trees as the willow, the palm and the myrtle and in the Talmud called it the "lulav". The "goodly" tree bough they defined as a citrus and called it the "etrog". **The citrus is thought to represent the Tree of the Knowledge of Good and Evil from the Garden of Eden.**[81]

It has been observed that, in the lulav, the palm branch has edible fruit, but no aroma. This would seem to symbolize that there are some in Israel who have knowledge of God's Word but do not have good works.

The myrtle branch has aroma but has no edible fruit. This would seem to symbolize that there are some in Israel who have good works but have no knowledge of God's Word.

The willow has neither aroma nor edible fruit. This would seem to symbolize that there are some in Israel who have neither knowledge of the Word of God nor good works.

The etrog or citrus branch has both aroma and good fruit. Rabbis think this symbolizes those in Israel who have both knowledge of the Word of God and good works. A Gentile observation might be that the citrus, which was introduced into Israel in later times, might symbolize the

Gentile Church. It is added to the lulav, which symbolizes Israel, or as some might say, grafted in, and the whole bundle of boughs used to worship and praise God. What a perfect picture, I think, of the Millennium when both Jew and Gentile will join together to worship the King of Kings and Lord of Lords.

- **All Jews must dwell in "booths" or outdoor huts during the 7 day feast.**

God instructed the Jews to build tabernacles or booths outdoors and live in them during this feast time. The booths are built of tree branches or of whatever materials that are available. The only requirement is that the stars at night must be visible through the roof and that the roof be constructed of something that grew from the earth. The roof would also allow some rain to enter but should shade most of the sunlight. In actual practice, the booths might be constructed in a back yard or if there was not room, on the rooftop of the house. It might be against the side of the house and have only three walls. The construction was a family activity with even the smallest members of the family participating. The booth was made as beautiful as could be and was decorated with all kinds of natural decorations as well as rugs, tapestries and all kinds of man made decorations. It was a fun activity for the whole family and started a week of rejoicing and feasting.[82] The Feast of Tabernacles/Booths is a picture of the Millennium or Messianic Kingdom when Jesus Christ will dwell and reign on the earth.

# ACTIONS

## Sacrifices are offered.  Numbers 29:12-39

As we read the abundance of sacrifices listed in the scriptures above that are offered in this feast day, a fascinating pattern begins to emerge.  Seventy bullocks were offered on the altar.  These 70 bullocks seem to have a connection to the 70 nations of Zechariah 14:16-19 which will come to Jerusalem to worship during the Millennium.  There were also 70 people who came to Egypt when Jacob took his family there to escape the famine in Exodus 1:1-5.

Another fascinating pattern is in the 182 sacrifices offered during the week.  The 182 sacrifices and each of the groupings broken down in the scriptures are evenly divisible by 7. (Get your Bible and calculator and check it out.) It is a 7 day feast, occurring in the 7th month and all of the sacrifices are evenly divisible by 7.  God seems to be using His perfect number to show us a perfect picture of His Perfect Plan.

## Build and dwell in huts or booths.

The booths symbolize man living in an environment where the Light of the World can enter, where the wind of the Holy Spirit comes in freely, and the Latter Day rains can penetrate the dwelling.  What a perfect picture of the Millennium.

## Rejoice

Rejoice!!  God Reigns and dwells in fellowship with mankind forever more!!

# CHAPTER NINE ENDNOTES

78. Revelation 20:2

79. Jude 1:14, 1 Thessalonians 3:13, 1 Corinthians 6:2.

80. Materials from *"The Seven Festivals of the Messiah"*, by Edward Chumney, copyright 1994, used by permission of Destiny Image Publishers, 167 Walnut Bottom Road, Shippensburg, PA 17257 www.destinyimage.com

81. Mitch and Zhava Glasner, *The Fall Feasts of Israel*, p 190-193, © 1987 Reprinted by permission from Moody Publishers of Chicago

82. Mitch and Zhava Glasner, *The Fall Feasts of Israel*, p 187-188, Moody Press, © 1987 Moody Bible Institute of Chicago

# CHAPTER TEN

## WRAPPING IT ALL UP
### AN OVERVIEW

I have spent most of my life as a rancher in the rough, brush infested Palo Pinto Hill Country of North Central Texas. Most of our family-owned ranchland is rocky, cedar covered terrain that makes it extremely difficult to locate and care for livestock. Early in life, out of necessity, I learned the art of tracking livestock. It's different from the way the movies portray it. They portray it as an Indian or outdoorsman with some kind of supernatural ability to follow every step of the one being tracked. In actual practice, following the trail of an animal doesn't always work that way. There are areas where every step of the animal can be traced, but soon an area is encountered where the ground is so hard or rocky that footprints cannot be detected. When such an area is encountered, the procedure is to make a circle in the direction that the tracks were moving and try to pick up the trail again farther on. By doing this repeatedly, one begins to establish a direction the animal is moving and soon begins to suspect strongly where the animal is heading such as a feed plot, water hole or just a cool bedding spot where the wind will blow away the flies. As one begins to understand the habits of this particular animal, one can often leave the trail and go directly to the suspected destination without following every twist and turn of the trail.

That is the way I regard the Roadmap of God's Plan for Mankind. It is often not possible to track God every step of the way, but one doesn't have to follow the Roadmap for very long until one has a strong suspicion of the destination. In places the trail is very plain, but in other places it is not distinct. Then just when one thinks one has lost the trail, it become very distinct again and, from an overall view, is still heading for the destination.

Let's back off and get an overall view of God's work with mankind through recorded history and see if the roadmap or trail we are following involving the feasts is still there.

- God created Adam on Rosh Hashanah or the first day of the Jew's Secular calendar.

- The first Passover was set up and the Passover lamb killed and his blood painted over the doorposts to protect those inside. Centuries later, Jesus was crucified on that feast day at exactly the time the lamb was slain in the Passover ceremony. By applying Jesus' blood to the doorposts of our lives through faith, we have eternal protection.

- God led Jacob and his family into Egypt to escape from the famine exactly 430 years to the day before Moses led their descendents who had multiplied

**176**

into a nation out of Egypt as related in the book of Exodus. This day later became the first day of the Feast of Unleavened Bread and was the exact day Jesus lay in the grave after His Crucifixion.

• God caused the Ark to strike ground on the 17th day of the 7th month of the Jew's Secular calendar. Centuries later, God split the Red Sea and allowed Moses and the Jews to pass over on dry ground on that exact day. About 40 years later, it was the exact day that the Jews ate of the firstfruits of the Promised Land and became the Feast of Firstfruits. When transferred to the Jew's new calendar as set up in Exodus, this date became the exact day that Jesus arose still more centuries later.

• Moses went up the mountain to receive the stone tablets written by the Hand of God on the day that was to become the Feast of Pentecost. Centuries later, the Holy Spirit was given to the New Testament Church in Jerusalem on the exact anniversary of that day.

After these events, the trail grows cold again, but we have established a pattern: God is causing these major events in His Work with man to occur exactly on feast days. Four of the seven feasts have been fulfilled by a New Testament event exactly on a feast day and in the exact order of the feasts. What major events does the New Testament tell us are still in the future?

1. The rapture or catching away of the Church. (Theme of Rosh Hashanah/Feast of Trumpets)

2.  The physical coming of Jesus to set up His reign in Jerusalem.  (Theme of Yom Kippur/Day of Atonement)

3.  The Millennial Reign of Jesus over all the earth. (Theme of Feast of Tabernacles/Booths)

Since the themes of each of these unfulfilled fall feasts have a theme matching these events exactly, and since the fulfilled spring feasts were fulfilled exactly on feast days, I think we can predict that these future events will occur on exactly a feast day in the future.  I believe that is where the trail is leading and that our Roadmap is there.

Earlier in the book, I cautioned against "date setting".  That is not what I'm doing now.  I do not know in what **year** the next event will occur but I believe the pattern clearly indicates that when it does occur, **it will occur on a feast day**.  I also think the indications are that it will be **soon.**

I know that for generations, believers have thought that the rapture would occur in their lifetime.  The early Church in Acts thought so also.  Peter spoke of the times they were living in as the "last days". That was 2,000 years ago.  I think we could safely call our times the "last of the last days."  Why would we think that in the times in which we live the rapture is more imminent than 100 years ago? We have a very good reason for believing this.  **That rea-son is Israel.**  The Jews are back in the land after 2,500+ years and fulfill prophecy of events that the Bible says will happen in the end times.  We are the generation that has seen these events happen.  We have passed the last trail markers when we saw the establishment of Israel as a nation again after 2,500+ years in 1948 and when we saw the return of Jerusalem to Jewish control during the 6 day war of 1967. **<u>The last of the last days are now!!</u>**

You may not agree with me that the rapture could occur during our generation and that we are the last generation before the return of Jesus for His Church, but one thing is certain: this is yours and my last generation. We are each only one heartbeat and one breath away from meeting The Lord. The Bible plainly states:

*And as it is appointed unto men once to die, but after this the judgment.*

(Hebrews 9:27 AV)

How can we prepare for this judgment whether it be at the rapture or at death?

Don't depend on my opinion, or for that matter, any other man's opinion for the answer to that question. It's

far too important a decision to base on any other information except God's Word as revealed to us in the Bible.
Here's what God's Word, the Holy Bible, says about us as
mankind and how we can be righteous and acceptable to a
Holy God.

> *For all have sinned, and come short of the glory*
> *of God.*
>
> (Romans 3:23 AV)

> *As it is written, There is none righteous, no, not*
> *one.*
>
> (Romans 3:10 AV)

> *But we are all as an unclean [thing], and all our*
> *righteousnesses [are] as filthy rags; and we all do*
> *fade as a leaf; and our iniquities, like the wind,*
> *have taken us away.*
>
> (Isaiah 64:6 AV)

All men have sinned. That means you, me and every
other man or woman who ever walked on this earth. That
sin, whether it be just one or many, disqualifies us from fellowship with God. You may have sinned less than someone
else, but God doesn't grade on the curve. We are all sinners.

> *For the wages of sin [is] death; but the gift of God*
> *[is] eternal life through Jesus Christ our Lord.*
>
> (Romans 6:23 AV)

> *But God commendeth his love toward us, in that,*
> *while we were yet sinners, Christ died for us.*
>
> (Romans 5:8 AV)

Because we are sinners, we are under a death sentence.
This means not only physical death but spiritual death as

well. Spiritual death is eternal separation from God. Our hope is that God has provided a way for us to escape this death sentence. Jesus (who was God in the flesh) came and died on the cross to pay the debt of the death sentence we owed. This is a free gift that is offered by God to anyone who will accept it.

> *For God so loved the world, that he gave his only begotten Son, that whosoever believeth in him should not perish, but have everlasting life.*
> (John 3:16 AV)

> *That if thou shalt confess with thy mouth the Lord Jesus, and shalt believe in thine heart that God hath raised him from the dead, thou shalt be saved. For with the heart man believeth unto righteousness; and with the mouth confession is made unto salvation.*
> (Romans 10:9-10 AV)

> *For whosoever shall call upon the name of the Lord shall be saved.*
> (Romans 10:13 AV)

Any gift that is offered must be either rejected or received. To do nothing is to reject it, but if you know you have not believed and called on Him as your Savior or if you are not sure of your relationship with God, you can accept His Gift right now in the privacy of your own will. It's as simple as ABC.

**A. ADMIT:** Lord Jesus, I know I'm a sinner. I'm sorry for my sins and, with your help, I want to turn from them.

**B. BELIEVE:** Lord Jesus, I believe you are the Son of God. I believe you came in the flesh to live the perfect life I could not live. I believe you died on the cross to pay for <u>my</u> sins and arose again the third day and you are now alive.

**C. CALL**: Lord Jesus, I call on your name to save me. I believe you have come into my heart, right now. Amen.

You have just done what God's Word, The Bible, says to become a born again follower of Christ. Your future home is heaven. You have many privileges here on earth. Find out what they are.

Second Corinthians 5:17 says:

*Therefore if any man be in Christ, he is a new creature: old things are passed away; behold, all things are become new.*

As a new creature, you should go to the next step to show God that you are sincere.

**D. DEMONSTRATE** what has happened in your life.

**Tell** someone what has happened to you.

**Show it** by publicly professing Christ in your church and being baptized.

**Study** His Word.

**Expect** His Return.

*182*

Thanks for reading the things God has shown me about the feasts. If we never personally get to meet in this life here on earth, I **will** see you in the fall when Jesus comes for His Church. It may even be this fall.

I'll leave you with the old saying that used to be heard among cowboys working the roundups:

**"I'll see you in the fall,**
**If I see you at all."**

**Until then, May God Bless.**

# ABOUT THE AUTHOR

Jim Kelly is a third generation career rancher whose family-owned ranch is located in the Palo Pinto Hill Country of North Central Texas. Now semi-retired, he and his wife, Josie, operate Salt and Light Ministries, a not for profit prison and counseling ministry corporation. They both have served some 13 years as Volunteer Chaplains in the Texas Department of Criminal Justice. In addition, Josie also is a Texas Licensed Professional Counselor with a practice in the North Texas area. They live in solitude on the ranch, over a mile from the nearest neighbor, 16 miles from the nearest town and several miles from even their mailbox.

Jim has had a long and varied career in the business world and through the years has been the owner of a livestock feed business, an electrical contractor, commercial pilot, free lance writer of outdoor stories, hunting guide and outfitter, automobile service business owner, and has even found time to serve two terms as a Texas Justice of the Peace as well as operating a lifelong cattle ranching operation.

Jim traveled for many years as a revival preparation man for several evangelists based in Texas and Oklahoma as well as teaching Bible studies, lay preaching, and holding almost every church office known at one time or another.  After the death of his 29 year-old only son to a drug related suicide in 1993, Jim has devoted much time and study to ministry in drug and alcohol rehabilitation units in the Texas Prison System.  He is an ordained non-denominational minister with a passion for using God's Word to help men and women break free from drug addiction and the drug lifestyle.  He preaches and teaches regularly at prison units and occasionally churches in the North Texas area.

# PRE-PUBLICATION REVIEWS:-

## FROM THE AUTHOR AND TEACHER THAT SPARKED MY INTEREST IN THE FEASTS.

Rabbi Samuel Raphael Hirsch has suggested that the "Jew's catechism is his calendar." And for the Jew, "Pattern is prophecy." The Apostle Paul also emphasized that

*Whatsoever things were written aforetime were written for our learning.*

(Romans 15:4)

One of the most fruitful studies that a Christian can undertake is to discover the details behind the Mosaic feasts, and Jim Kelly's book is a great way to start. From their historical roots to their prophetic relevance, it is a tour that will enrich your Biblical perspectives.

Dr. Chuck Missler- Koinonia House Inc.,
Coeur d'Alene, ID www.khouse.org

## MESSIANIC JEWISH MINISTRIES

Articulate and thorough exposition of the symbolism as related to the seven feasts and Pre-tribulation patterns. Insightful, interesting reading. The ideas are clear, and well presented.

Zola Levitt Ministries, Inc. www.levitt.com

Jim Kelly has done the community of faith an inestimable service. Carefully written and comprehensive in scope, he takes us on a journey, creating a *Roadmap* to understanding God's sovereign plan and purpose, for both Jew and Gentile alike. Kelly is a terrific guide, deftly leading the reader through each of God's "appointed times." Highly recommended as a balanced introduction to the feasts of Israel and their prophetic connection to our Messiah.

Steven Charles
Ger-Director/Sojourner Ministries,
Exploring the Jewish Heart of Christianity,
Garland, TX. www.sojournerministries.com

## PUBLISHER

Frankly, I do not recall reading such a well researched, well documented book on the 7 Feasts in my 33 years as a Christian. Thank you for having the impetus and strength to compile and publish this wonderful contribution to both Christian and Jewish literature.

Dr. Michael Wourms, President and Founder,
CSN Books. www.csnbooks.com

## PRISON MINISTRIES

Thank you Chaplain Kelly for writing such an excellent book on the Seven Feasts of Israel. We know that true change comes only through the Word of God and a personal relationship with Jesus Christ. This book will greatly help students of the Bible on their journey of spiritual transformation. It is presented in a clear, easy-to-understand way that new believers as well as mature Christians will enjoy.

Mike Barber, Mike Barber Ministries, Inc. www.mikebarber.org

Wow! Glory to God! *GOD'S ROADMAP FOR MAN: THE 7 FEASTS OF ISRAEL* will grab hold of you and pull you in. I found myself reading and rereading this great work as a powerful faith filled vision of hope and excitement emerged and illuminated my spirit.

Rev. Michael R. Holly
President/Founder Unchained Life Ministries, Inc.
www.unchainedlife.org

## PASTORS

When I was in Bible College I met a man with a passion for God and a passion for souls. Over the years I have watched Jim Kelly minister to hurting people on the mission fields of Fort Worth, Texas and the Navajo Indian Reservation. The book that is in your hand is a tool that has been crafted from the heart of an awesome man of God. Within this book lies the power to transform and sculpt a life unto Christ. This book is a must read for anyone breathing.

Kenton Pate- Senior Pastor,
Church for You, Watauga, TX.
www.churchforyou.net

It has been a joy to review this work on the 7 Feasts of Israel. Biblical accuracy is evident from beginning to end. A must for every pastor and believer with a desire to know the handiwork of God in the life of mankind.

Pastor Tom Moore,
First Assembly of God, Breckenridge, TX.

## CHAPLAINS

Jim Kelly has given us a study approach to the Bible that has either been missed or neglected by most of our Christian teachers and publishers. He has encouraged us to do our own study and be led by the Holy Spirit. Jim is a friend that I love, and I trust his sincerity in wanting to help men and women come to a knowledge of the truth.

Glenn Mitchell, Chaplain,
John Middleton Transfer Facility,
Texas Dept. of Criminal Justice.

I have always enjoyed holidays and family get-to-gathers. After reading the book I know that God has a specific design in the feast days. They are significant in God's plan and are not just happenstance; they have a purpose in the big picture. Now when the feasts come they have more meaning and I anticipate with expectancy the celebration.

Earnest Brown, Chaplain,
Walker-Sayle Unit,
Texas Dept. of Criminal Justice.